BARNW

12 Dec '23
7/3/25
1 1 AUG 2025

CW01543592

Cambridgeshire Libraries & Information Service

This book is due for return on or before the latest date shown above, but may be renewed up to three times unless it has been requested by another customer.

Books can be renewed -
in person at your local library
By phone **0345 045 5225**
  Monday to Saturday 8am-8pm
Online www.cambridgeshire.gov.uk/library

Please note that charges are made on overdue books.

Derek Booth

C0000 00194 4593

About the author

Derek Booth was born in Poole, Dorset in 1940, but at the age of one he went to Hastings, East Sussex, the home town of his parents. Perhaps living in Hastings associated with the famous battle of that name in 1066, as every school child is taught, instilled in Derek a sense of history.

After attending Hastings Grammar School, Derek went north to Hull University where he was awarded a B.Sc.(Hons.) in zoology and subsequently two Ph.D's (one from Hull) associated with a research career in reproductive biology, first within the medical field in London, then from 1965 in Cambridge concentrating on farm animals. Derek is a chartered Member of the Society of Biology.

A retirement interest is archaeology and local history supported by membership of the 174 year old Cambridge Antiquarian Society; Derek became a Vice President of the society. Derek has been the Parish Archaeological Warden for Milton, for over 10 years, and has previously produced two other books, one a semi-autobiography, 'Boy of the Wealden Shore', and a second with two other scientists, on the history of the station where breeding in farm animals was studied.

Derek working on a test pit in Hill Close, Milton.

First published in 2014 by Derek Booth

Copyright © Derek Booth

Email: booth30@btinternet.com

ISBN 978-0-9569026-1-0

A catalogue record of this book is available from the British Library.

Derek Booth has asserted his right to be identified as the author of this work. No part of this publication may be reproduced, transmitted or stored in a retrieval system in any form, or by any means, without written permission of the publisher.

All photographs and illustrations are in the ownership of the author except as otherwise indicated where copyright permission has been granted. Every effort has been made to trace and acknowledge ownership of copyright of illustrations in this book. The publisher will be pleased to make suitable arrangements to clear permission with any copyright holders whom it has not been possible to contact.

Printed in Great Britain by

impression IT
Unit 2
Maunsell Road
St Leonards - on - Sea
East Sussex
TN38 9NL

Tel: +44 (0) 1424 852116

www.impressionit.co.uk

front cover illustration: the old oak tree at Hill Close (off Fen Road), symbolizes the development of Milton, because it exists in an ancient landscape where people have lived and farmed down through the ages giving rise to the anecdote for Hill Close as 'the village'. The sawn off branch of the tree can be seen symbolically, as the end of an era of a predominantly farming village. The new branches thrust upwards with optimism for the new Milton, with its science based industries and educational institutions, while the country park and easy access to the River Cam provide excellent leisure facilities – the tree of life goes on.

"Knowing the past, illuminates the future"

Dedication

This book is dedicated to my wife Judith with whom I have shared 50 years of happy marriage, and to our two daughters, Rebecca and her family, and Catherine. Also to the memory of our eldest daughter Amanda, whose short presence denied her the advantages of living in Milton which the rest of the family have been able to appreciate to enrich our lives.

Contents

A note on illustrations

Acknowledgements

	Page
Preface	1
Introduction	4
1. The scene is set	8
2. First inhabitants	14
3. Romans everywhere	28
4. Anglo-Saxons – founders of Milton	56
5. Normans – 'still with us'	72
6. Land to the people	121
7. Farmstead to suburbia	146
8. Where from here?	177
Further reading	183
Some useful websites	188

A note on illustrations

Most of the maps found in the chapters, are sketch maps based on the boundaries of the parish of Milton, and include throughout features such as the old main village roads, and water courses such as the Milton brook. This water course starts at the western higher land in the village and meanders by the doctors' surgery, through Tomkin's Mead, under Old School Lane and Fen Road to the Humphrey Repton lake behind Milton Hall before tracking a course across Milton Fen to the River Cam. However, today, Milton brook is a remnant of its earlier status with water being absent, except after heavy rains, from many of the village stretches. The main railway line between Cambridge and Ely is shown, as is the old Cambridge and St Ives railway line, now the Guided Bus track forming the southern boundary of Milton parish. All these features are repeated in every sketch map together with the location of All Saints' Church. This base map has additions as appropriate to the context of the chapters (i.e. symbols for the location of archaeological artefacts, field boundaries and buildings etc.).

The sketch maps were drawn by the author, and the photographs were either taken by him, or others as indicated.

Acknowledgements

Inspiration to write this book, in part arose from my introduction to field archaeology through my involvement as a volunteer with the Cambridgeshire County Archaeologists over 15 years ago. However, during this time the main body of the County's field archaeologists has become commercialised and absorbed into one of the country's largest commercial archaeology groups Oxford Archaeology, as Oxford Archaeology East (OAE) based at Bar Hill. Some of the Cambridgeshire archaeologists remain employed by the County, while a few have joined other commercial groups. Therefore my gratitude for my training with the original staff of the County Archaeologists, is expressed in relation to their current employment positions.

My first exposure to archaeological artefacts was washing pottery sherds and bone arising from the County archaeologists' excavations in the Cambridge region, when they were based at Fulbourn. In 1998, I went on a training course being held by the County archaeologists at one of the many excavations under way at that time on the Landfill Site off Butt Lane, Milton. The project supervisor was Aileen Connor (now at OAE) who I am indebted to for this rigorous launch into field archaeology. Other excavations followed with introductions to many of the staff employed as County archaeologists. Among these are the following, all now employees at OAE who have offered me assistance for which I am extremely grateful, with archaeological techniques and artefact processing, identification and report writing: Steve Wadeson – Roman pottery, Carole Fletcher and Richard Mortimer – medieval pottery, David Crawford-White – co-ordinating the 6th forms in relation to fieldwalking, and Stephen Macaulay for his general interest and encouragement. Both David and Stephen were involved in their capacity as outreach officers associated with

Cambridgeshire Archaeology based at the Shire Hall complex.

Also at Shire Hall in the Cambridgeshire Archaeology Historic Environment Record (HER) Office, were the following staff who provided the detailed identification of metal finds: Sarah Poppy (now with English Heritage), Philippa Walton (now at the British Museum) and Lizzie Gill; for their assistance I am duly grateful. Other archaeologists employed by the County Council whose assistance receive my gratitude, are Quinton Carroll, the manager of the HER team including notably, Sally Croft, for their up-dating me with the archeological records for Milton, and Helen Fowler (OAE and now at the HER), as the Finds Liason Officer for the Portable Antiquities Scheme, for her role as a practical co-ordinator in the Milton fieldwalks involving the 6th form students. I also thank Mark Hinman (once of OAE, but now a key manager with Pre-construct Archaeology), for his assistance in the computation and display of some of the data from the fieldwalking projects at Hill Close and Long Meadow.

Lastly among the professional archaeologists who I wish to thank, is Trevor Ennis of Essex County Council Archaeology (now Archaeology Southeast), for allowing me access to the Bellway housing development site to observe the second phase of excavations behind Milton Hall.

Aside from the assistance of the professional archaeologists, were two voluntary groups who became engaged in the archaeology of Hill Close and Long Meadow; their involvement added that extra dimension to the projects. First, was Dr Brian Bridgland and Ian Sanderson of Archaeology RheeSearch with their team who carried out a geophysical survey of the fieldwalking sites which so effectively complemented the earlier aerial photography survey by Roger Palmer. Secondly, Michelle Bullivant and Graeme Clarke of Active 8 Archaeology with their volunteers, who carried out the test pit excavations on the fieldwalk sites. I am most grateful for the role of these two groups in contributing to the further archaeology of Milton.

My thanks also extend to John Wilson representing the landowners, and Bertram Pearson the tenant farmer (both men from old Milton families), for their permission to access Hill Close and Long Meadow, to carry out geophysical surveys, fieldwalks with metal detection, and test pits excavations.

Other sources of material which have contributed to a more complete story, have been old photographs and maps held at the Cambridgeshire Collection, Central Library, Cambridge, documents likewise found at the Cambridgeshire Record Office, and photographs of Roman finds at the Landfill Site, Milton taken by Alison Taylor; I am most grateful for their permission to reproduce this illustrative material. In addition, outside Cambridge, the Hertfordshire Archaeological Trust (now Archaeological Solutions Ltd), provided me with the reports on their excavations at All Saints' Church, Milton, and I am grateful for their permission to use material from this source.

Remaining thanks are due to the Cambridge Antiquarian Society for the provision of a grant towards the production of this book, also to John Davis of impression IT for his excellent professional skills in printing and compiling the work, and finally to my wife Judith for her most helpful comments and suggestions, and support in seeing this work through to completion.

Preface

The theme of this book is to trace the origins of the village of Milton situated on the southern edge of the Cambridgeshire fenlands, from prehistoric times to the present day. Particular reference is given to archaeological records, the landscape, architectural features, population and occupations of this rural fen edge village, important in history as part of the 'granary of England' with good road and river connections, yet situated only 3 miles from the centre of the ancient university city of Cambridge.

Rather than presenting the story as a plain descriptive monologue, the story develops through the 'novel' approach of a dialogue between fictional characters: a recently retired university don, Dr Charles Crowfoot (the author, transposed) and a 6th form student. The student Tom Barnes, receives weekly tutorials every Saturday morning over a period of 8 weeks, covering one historic period a week from Dr Crowfoot in relation to Tom's 'A' level archaeology course, and Tom's general interest in the history of Milton; the tutorials are held at Dr Crowfoot's home Kiln Cottage. The dialogue complements the overall descriptive factual text.

Conveniently, Dr Crowfoot and Tom live in Milton, and this makes it easier for Tom to visit Dr Crowfoot's cottage to receive an hour's tuition on a Saturday morning over 8 weeks in the autumn term of his first year in the 6th form. The purpose of the tutorials, is to provide Tom, who is new to the village and has a keen interest in the history and archaeology of Milton, with detailed information on the archaeology of Milton down through the ages; this provides a basis for an individual project as part of Tom's 'A' level course in archaeology. Each chapter represents one tutorial, and the significance of the dialogue between tutor and student, is that this medium allows for questions and answers, and comments between tutor and student around the topics being introduced. This adds interest, by the transfer of information to the reader wishing to know more about the actual archaeology of Milton in an historical context.

The story starts with the first tutorial, which sets the scene dealing with the meeting of a rather apprehensive Tom with Dr Crowfoot at Kiln Cottage in Fen Road; this is after a short cycle ride from Tom's parents' house in a new housing development in the village. On his arrival at Kiln Cottage, Tom is greeted by first a Siamese cat called Caesar, before meeting Dr Crowfoot at the front door. Tom is then led into a typical homely cottage lounge (reflecting the wide interests of Dr Crowfoot), with a warm log fire and Victorian upholstered chairs set either side of the fireplace for tutor and student. Soon to follow, are coffee and biscuits made by Mrs Crowfoot, before Dr Crowfoot outlines the programme for the weekly tutorials. By now, Tom feels more relaxed and filled with enthusiasm to take on the challenge in the coming weeks, that of finding out about the development of his village through archaeological finds, landscape changes and architectural features of buildings, notably the parish church of All Saints', and the people who have lived in Milton.

Each chapter starts with variations on the theme of Tom waking up on the Saturday morning of his tutorial, and subsequently arriving at Dr Crowfoot's cottage where he receives his welcoming refreshments before the start of his tutorial.

After the introductory chapter dealing with setting the scene, there are six chapters (tutorials) concerned with the time sequence of prehistory, the Romans, Anglo-Saxons and Vikings, the Normans through to the end of the 18th century, but including All Saints' church into the 21st century, the significance of the Enclosure Act to the 19th century, and the 20th century dealing with the conversion of farm land to industry, embracing sand and gravel extraction, small light industry, science based industry and the Science Park, and leisure with the Milton Country Park. This evolution of Milton results in significant changes in land use, population and occupations. The final period embraces improvements to road infrastructure linked to the expansion of non-land based industries, and the expansion of housing and the population as Milton becomes a suburban village virtually annexed to the city of Cambridge.

The last chapter gazes into the crystal ball to see what career opportunities might be open for a student like Tom with interests in archaeology, and what archaeology there might still be hidden, waiting to be discovered to reveal more about Milton's long and fascinating history important to the economy of the nation.

It is important to note that the dialogue only applies to the fictional characters Dr Crowfoot, his wife, his cat Caesar, the name of his cottage and garden, and the other main character, Tom Barnes; there is a brief mention of Tom's parents in the last chapter. The remainder of the text with reference to people and places, is the monologue component of fact about the history, archaeology and architecture of Milton through time.

Dr Crowfoot is named after an aquatic plant called Water Crowfoot *(Ranunculus aquatilis)* which is found in still waters, streams and rivers – typical of a fenland landscape.

Introduction

A visit to the Cambridgeshire Collection at the Cambridgeshire Library in Cambridge City, will immediately reveal the wealth of books concerned with the history of many villages in Cambridgeshire. These books have been compiled by enthusiastic local historians, and a notable example is 'The Common Stream', written by Rowland Parker. Rowland, a schoolteacher and inhabitant of the village of Foxton a few miles south of Cambridge, published his book in the mid-1970's and its was so successful that reprinted copies were produced. In essence, Rowland Parker's book is a 'broad brush' of content ranging from topography including the small stream around which old Foxton has developed through time, to archaeological features related to the various peoples who have lived in the Foxton area from prehistory to the 20th century. Each historical period is highlighted with reference to character studies of those involved in the many aspects of village life. But it is not just 'flesh and blood' which makes the history of the village, where people lived and worked is also important; buildings and their architecture complete the portrait of the evolution of this distinctive English village.

I had often considered writing a book on the history of my village Milton in Cambridgeshire, where I have lived with my family for nearly 50 years of my adult life. However, although this seems a long time, not being born a native of Milton, I felt that I did not have sufficient personal contacts with the true natives of the village, to acquire those particularly interesting stories about the diverse people belonging to the many old Milton families. A living representative of one of these families would make a better contribution to the social history of the village, than me, I am sure!

There was already an existing historical compilation of Milton, written by the Rev William Keating Clay in 1869 which gave rise to his book, 'A History of the Parish of Milton in the County of Cambridge' (Clay also wrote similar histories on Landbeach, Waterbeach and Horningsea). However, these works were primarily concerned with the parish churches of these villages. A more general history including archaeological aspects, was produced as a relatively small article by Ken Humpries in 1962, called 'The Story of Milton'. Ken was a resident of Milton, a local historian and a parish and South Cambridgeshire District councillor; he is remembered by having two roads named after him in the newer housing developments of the village viz. Ken's Way and Humphries Way. Finally, there was the Victoria County History for Cambridgeshire and the Isle of Ely, volume 9, 1989, which includes the most detailed historical information for Milton. So, how could I contribute to writing about the history of Milton?

The question was answered for me eight years ago, when I was involved as the parish archaeological warden for Milton with the then Cambridgeshire County archaeologists, and students from Hills Road 6th form college and the Perse 6th form, on fieldwalks to the north of Fen Road in Milton; farmworkers and I, had previously found Roman pottery sherds scattered at random across the fields. The students were studying archaeology at 'A' level, and the fieldwalks were a practical part of the course. The outcome of these fieldwalks, was that they resulted in a considerable quantity of Roman and medieval pottery finds. These together with features revealed by earlier aerial photography, geophysical surveys, and metal objects including coins by voluntary metal detecting groups found at the same time as the fieldwalks, revealed the site of a Romano-British farmstead and the first notable archaeology for the supposed site of a medieval manor house. Later, small excavations, supported these conclusions. A bonus of the surveys, was pottery and metal finds, constituting the first archaeological evidence for the Anglo-Saxons being present not far from the parish church of All Saints', and therefore also near the centre of the village as we know it today. These Germanic settlers would have been the founders of the village of Milton.

Being a retired agricultural scientist with an interest and practical experience in archaeology as a retirement hobby, the above mentioned finds inspired me to bring together, for the first time, all the reported archaeological data for the parish of Milton, and fit this into a story expanded to include historical evidence which traced the development of this historically significant village, Milton, through time. But, rather than writing a story as a monologue of facts, I thought it would make more interesting reading if the facts were delivered through a dialogue. This would involve on the one hand, a fictitious retired university teacher living in an equally fictitious cottage off Fen Road in Milton, while on the other hand, a fictitious 6th form student studying 'A' level archaeology and history with an additional interest in the local history of Milton would receive extra coaching from the retired university teacher.

The story unravels as the retired don, Dr Crowfoot, provides Tom Barnes the student, with a tutorial every Saturday morning at his cottage over a period of 8 weeks in the autumn term of Tom's first year in the 6th form. After Tom completes his tutorials, the story concludes with Dr Crowfoot visiting Tom and his parents at their house in a newer housing development area of Milton on the Sunday afternoon following the last tutorial the day before. The purpose of this get together is to discuss further education and training beyond 'A' levels and career prospects in archaeology, the main options being a field archaeologist, an archivist, a teacher in a school or in further and higher education, or museum work.

As Dr Crowfoot is about to leave Tom and his parents, he makes one final comment, that Tom's enthusiasm and motivation should place him in a good position to eventually obtain an employment suited to all the effort he has made in his chosen subjects of archaeology and history, particularly with reference to his own village.

It is a hope that those who read this story will likewise be inspired to become interested in the archaeology and history of Milton in Cambridgeshire (or indeed any other location), which has, and continues to be a significant settlement for human activity and productivity; Milton is certainly a part of Britain at the forefront of economic and cultural development in the 21st century.

1. The scene is set

It was a cool, Saturday morning in early October, when Tom Barnes awoke and felt nervous at the prospect of attending his first tutorial with Dr Charles Crowfoot on the archaeology in relation to the origins of Milton. After a light breakfast, he left his parents house, opened the door of the garden shed and retrieved his bicycle. However, as he cycled out along the road of the new housing development in an easterly direction towards the High Street in Milton, already the rising sun warmed Tom's cheeks, just a little, to add to the warmth beginning to circulate throughout his body as his legs likewise circulated the pedals. This burst of energy started to clear the 'cob webs' from Tom's head and his nervousness faded away to be replaced by a more confident enthusiasm as he entered Fen Road. Tom was on his way to visit Dr Charles Crowfoot, known to Tom's parents, and a retired university lecturer who gave talks on archaeology and local history to village organisations. But this morning, visiting Dr Crowfoot, was going to be an introduction to provide Tom, over a period of two months, with an hour's tutorial on Saturday mornings. This extra coaching was aimed at improving Tom's prospects of obtaining acceptable results at the end of his 'A' level course in archaeology being studied at a local 6th form college; the course included completing an individual project – Tom's was going to be on the archaeology of Milton.

About half way down Fen Road between the High Street and Milton Fen, through which the River Cam flows north, the time was now approaching 9.00 am when Tom dismounted from his bicycle at a small white gate with patches of peeling paint, set midway between two clipped hedgerows of hawthorn. Tom with difficulty, had to push the gate hard as it jammed on the brick path to allow himself, and his bicycle to proceed up the path towards the front door of Kiln Cottage. The cottage was a typical

Cambridge yellow brick building with a slate roof, built sometime in the middle of the 19th century.

As Tom approached the solid front door protected by years of successive coats of dark green paint, he was greeted by a sleek Siamese cat who eyed Tom suspiciously with a knowing look, implying that he had not previously encountered this intruder on his master's property. Tom leaned over, making the usual squeaking sounds with his lips that people emit when meeting a cat, and timidly stroked the smooth, buff coated feline – this immediately triggered an accepting response from the animal as he elevated his thin, brown tail to the vertical and started purring.

This friendly introduction to Kiln Cottage was followed by Tom lifting the heavy, black, iron knocker on the door and banging it down three times; after a few seconds, an inner door could be seen opening, as light from the back of the cottage passed through the house, creating a silhouette of the inner door visible through the small diamond window in the front door – someone was coming, then the front door opened. "Good morning Tom, that's a good start, you are very punctual," said Dr Crowfoot, a lean man with swept-back white hair, trimmed white beard, penetrating blue eyes and arched eyebrows. "Good morning Dr Crowfoot," replied Tom. Then Dr Crowfoot spoke with an assuring voice, "Please come in and let the cat in with you; Caesar is anxious to receive his breakfast – oh, and put your bicycle against the wall at the side of the cottage, it will be safe there" - the ice was broken. Dr Crowfoot led Tom through the small dark hallway into a comfortable looking room on the left. To Tom, Dr Crowfoot had the countenance of one who had seen many more years than his tutors at school, and likely to possess just that bit more specialist knowledge since he had been a university lecturer.

Dr Crowfoot pointed to a mahogany chair upholstered with gold velvet situated on the right of a fire place with a black iron surround. "Make yourself comfortable here," said Dr Crowfoot with a calm, but assured voice. A log fire had obviously only been lit recently as there were no glowing embers, but an array of vibrant warming flames; this was to be Tom's seat for the course of his tutorials. Dr Crowfoot then shuffled out of the room, Caesar following at his ankles as he went to the kitchen at the back of the house. Tom could hear voices coming from the kitchen as he glanced around his 'new lecture room' – an oil lamp perched on a small table, oil paintings around the walls (landscapes, and portraits perhaps of Dr Crowfoot's earlier relatives), family photographs, Persian rugs and two large book cupboards with glass doors set in the recesses either side of the fire place – the range of titles on the spines of the books covered so many subjects, ancient history and archaeology to natural history, art, philosophy, music, fly fishing, and gardening to name a few.

The voices Tom heard were that of Dr Crowfoot arranging with his wife to prepare some coffee and making sure that Caesar's insatiable appetite was being satisfied. Dr Crowfoot then re-entered the room, placed a tray of coffee and biscuits on a table near to Tom, and then sat in another Victorian gentleman's chair to the left of the fire place.

By this time, with a cup of coffee warming Tom's cold hands as they encased the cup, and consuming a wholesome home made biscuit, the result of Mrs Crowfoot's labours in the kitchen, Tom felt relaxed and ready for his tutorial. After a few minutes consuming the refreshments and an informal conversation about living in Milton, Dr Crowfoot switched the conversation to a formal mode to remind Tom why he was here on a Saturday morning.

Dr Crowfoot started to outline the programme for the tutorials, each lasting an hour from 9.00 – 10.00 am. The whole course of tutorials would deal with the development of Milton through time, from prehistory to the present day, with an emphasis on archaeological aspects in relation to an historical context. This information would be most useful for choosing an individual project from within Tom's 'A' level course in archaeology, and the reason why Tom had chosen Milton as his topic. But, in addition, with Tom and his family being new to Milton and Tom having a keen interest in the history of his village, it was because of this interest that Tom was going to receive more information from Dr Crowfoot than required for his 'A' level course. Tom was now in the right place with a conducive atmosphere, and he was overwhelmed with enthusiasm to be receptive to his first tutorial on the prehistory of Milton which would be next Saturday's lesson.

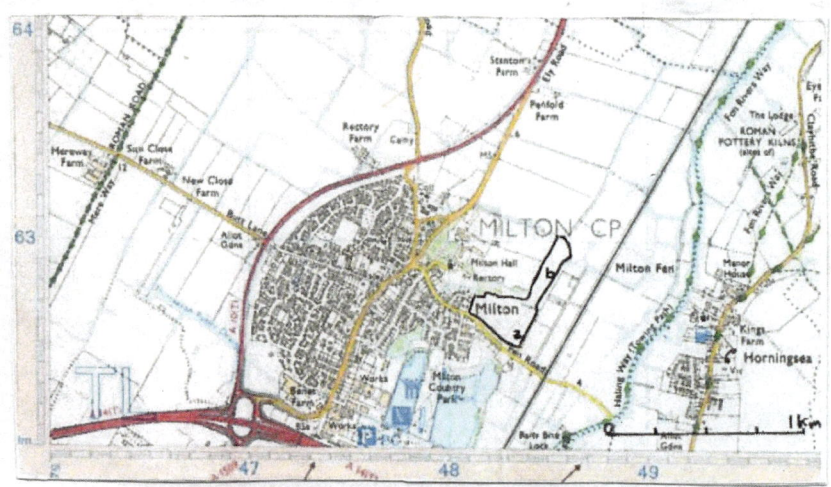

1. The village of Milton: (O.S. Map 2000, 1: 25000). © *Crown copyright*.

2. Aerial photograph of Milton: (a) is Hill Close – 'the Village' (finds: prehistoric, Romano-British, Anglo-Saxon and 13th century Manor House); (b) is Long Meadow – the Romano-British settlement (finds predominantly Romano-British). [Get Mapping plc]

3. View north to site of Romano-British farmstead at Long Meadow. Note green grass (central left) marking the old course of the Milton brook which formed the Humphrey Repton lake in the parkland of Milton Hall behind the trees.

4. Milton brook concealed by reeds, meanders northeast from Long Meadow across the Fen to the River Cam.

2. First inhabitants

Tom glanced at his watch, it was just approaching 9.00 am as he dismounted from his bike and wheeled it up the path to Kiln Cottage to its parking place at the side of the cottage as previously instructed by Dr Crowfoot. This Saturday morning, unlike a week ago when Tom was a little apprehensive about the extra coaching he was going to receive from Dr Crowfoot for his 'A' level archaeology project, he was now feeling confident and enthusiastic about this new Saturday morning commitment.

With coffee and biscuits consumed, Dr Crowfoot began to introduce Tom to his first tutorial which would be on the first inhabitants of Milton. "But," Dr Crowfoot emphasized, "before the people, comes the land, why should people want to live in this distinctive part of what is now the fen-edge of south Cambridgeshire?" Dr Crowfoot then proceeded to answer this question by giving an account of the underlying geology of the landscape and the merits of this for human habitation.

Topography and Geology

The present parish of Milton is essentially a square of around 830 hectares with the western boundary being the Roman road (Akeman Street or the Mere Way – the latter name will be used in future reference to this ancient trackway). The southern boundary is the old railway line from Cambridge to Huntingdon (now partly converted to the Guided Bus track), while the northern boundary is more erratic due to the field boundaries with the parishes of Landbeach and Waterbeach being slightly irregular. Finally, the eastern boundary of Milton parish is the winding River Cam, and it is from this area westwards that the geology of Milton is best realized.

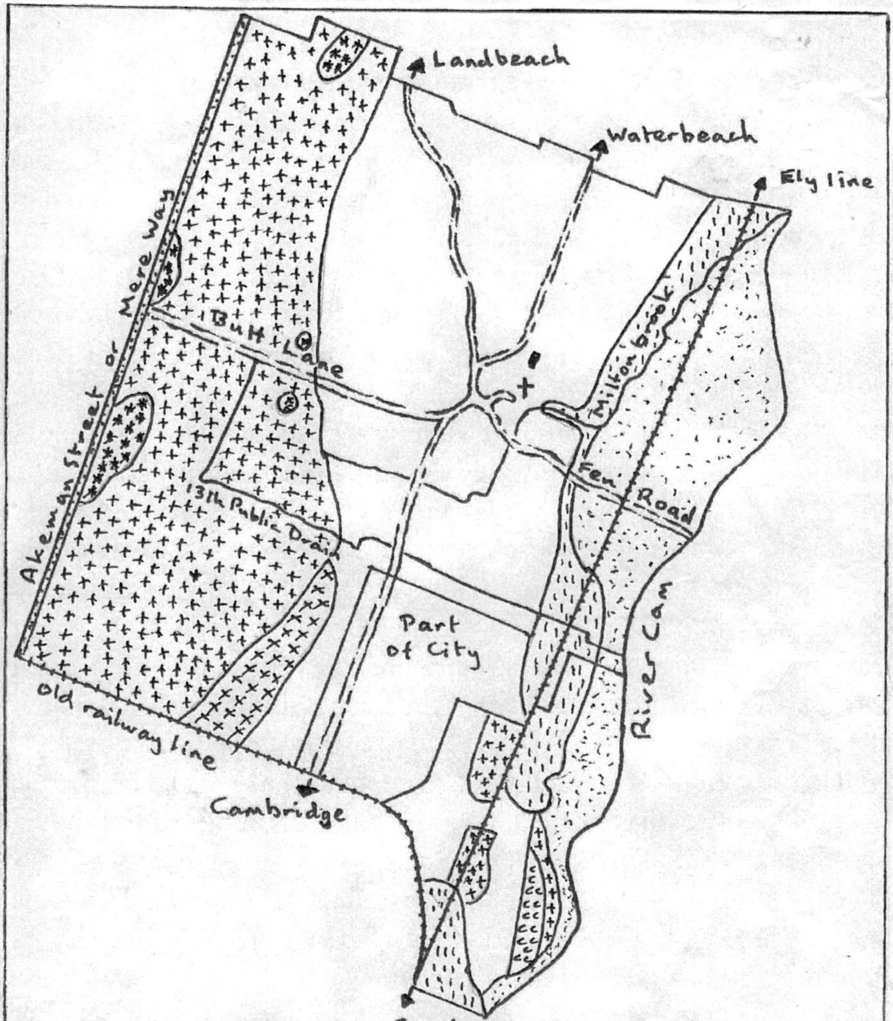

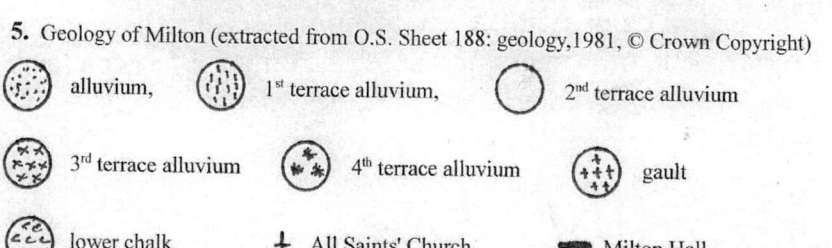

5. Geology of Milton (extracted from O.S. Sheet 188: geology, 1981, © Crown Copyright)

- alluvium,
- 1st terrace alluvium,
- 2nd terrace alluvium
- 3rd terrace alluvium
- 4th terrace alluvium
- gault
- lower chalk
- All Saints' Church
- Milton Hall

The River Cam itself, flows through fine alluvium forming a river basin and Milton Fen. This basin is bounded on the west side by a narrow terrace of sand and gravel (1st terrace alluvium) which then rises to a broad area of deep sand and gravel called 2nd terrace alluvium – around half of the landscape on which present day Milton village has developed. Underneath this Pleistocene cap of sand and gravel is Jurassic gault clay which comes to the surface westwards of the village before the Mere Way. It is from here that the 13th Public Drain and Milton brook arise. The latter then gathers more water as it flows east under the Cambridge Road, alongside Cole's Road into Tompkin's Mead, under Old School Lane and Fen Road to form the lake in Milton Hall grounds. The brook finally runs out to Milton Fen to meet the River Cam near the boundary with Waterbeach parish. Today, the Brook has little water due to its catchment being diverted to modern drainage channels associated with housing development. Over the gault clay in the west of the parish, there are a few caps of further sand and gravel constituting a 3rd and 4th terrace alluvium (illustration 5, after O.S. Sheet 188: geology, 1981, © *Crown copyright).*

Already Tom was beginning to see that the Milton landscape formed over 100,000 years ago, had attributes for human settlement, and Dr Crowfoot was soon to confirm Tom's developing thoughts. First, one access feature to the land was the river once people constructed boats. Then the land was ideally suited for growing crops including grass to feed animals with the sandy soil providing good drainage and the underlying gault clay having a complementary water holding property. Later, in time, the clay would be exploited for making pottery, bricks and tiles. Furthermore, and of prime importance, the climate was conducive to agriculture without undesirable extremes.

Stone Age

Dr Crowfoot then defined an important aspect of this day's tutorial to Tom, it was that the first inhabitants of Milton were not able to read or write and therefore could not record their experiences of life in this way, this is why this period in human civilization is called the prehistoric – before a written history. The earliest part of the prehistoric period with reference to Milton, is the Palaeolithic (Old Stone Age). From this time, was the finding of a mammoth's tusk and a tooth during gravel extractions off Fen Road in 1962, a site near the present entrance to the Country Park on this road.

Palaeolithic people (700,000 – 11,000 BP), were hunter - gatherers of nature's food sources, and generally were always on the move with little fixed settlements other than in caves – not part of the geology in this part of Cambridgeshire. These people were the first to produce tools from flakes of flint, or from bone or antlers, and would have caught fish including eels from the river and hunted land animals such as deer, wild cattle and pigs as well as wild fowl present in the marshland around the river, or in the dense woods on the higher land. Perhaps the remains of the mammoth found in Milton, were the 'left overs' of a hunted animal over 30,000 years ago, even killed by a Neanderthal man competing for his food with modern man *Homo sapiens*; or perhaps it just died of natural causes?

Dr Crowfoot's face then started to 'light up' as his eyebrows became more arched and his eyes twinkled, "Tom," he said, "We have now come to the stage in prehistory when we start to find the first artefacts made by people living in Milton; these artefacts are from the period following the Palaeolithic i.e. the Mesolithic (Middle Stone Age), (10,000 – 5,500 BP) and the Neolithic (New Stone Age) (4,000 – 2,500 BC). During these periods, farming for ready available food from plants and animals came into being together with more refined flint tools, and later, pottery for cooking the food being produced, but generally, settlements were

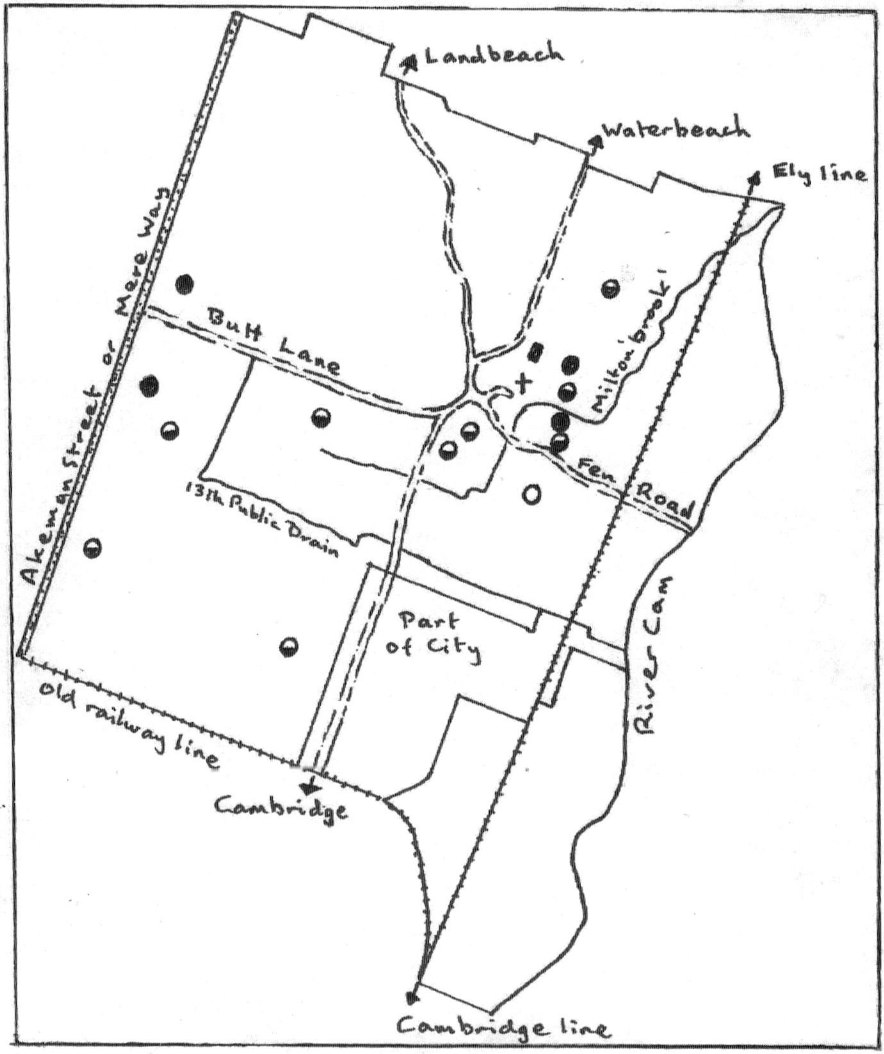

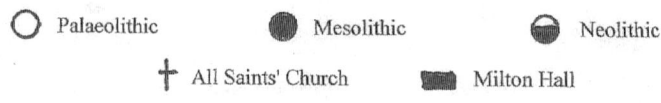

6. Stone Age distribution of finds.

○ Palaeolithic ● Mesolithic ◐ Neolithic

✝ All Saints' Church ▮ Milton Hall

temporary."

"But," Dr Crowfoot exclaimed, " before we look at these periods in the prehistory of Milton, there is one very important aspect which has allowed us to acquire archaeological data for these and later periods of Milton's history i.e. the development and expansion of the Landfill Site for Cambridge's solid waste to the south of Butt Lane during the last 20 years or so." Before Dr Crowfoot could say more, Tom, curious to know who carried out the archaeological work, interjected and said, "Dr Crowfoot, did you get involved in any of the archaeological field work?" Dr Crowfoot whimsically replied, "Well Tom, yes I did, both as a volunteer, and from time to time also able to offer some professional comments on the nature of the finds. The archaeological group I was working with was the Cambridgeshire County Council's Archaeological Field Unit based at Fulbourn, but later they moved to Bar Hill to become a more commercialized unit with development archaeology as CAMARC, before finally being absorbed into the national commercial archaeological organisation called Oxford Archaeology, as Oxford Archaeology East (OAE)". Dr Crowfoot then went on to inform Tom where and what was found in relation to the Mesolithic and Neolithic peoples arriving in Milton.

Sir Cyril Fox - archaeologist

But first, Dr Crowfoot digressed at this stage in the tutorial by referring to the 'bible' of Cambridgshire's archaeology written in the 1920's by Sir Cyril Fox. The written work, based on Cyril Fox's PhD thesis submitted to Cambridge University, was called 'The Archaeology of the Cambridge Region' and it is a synthesis of archaeological finds known at that time in this region. The book should be the first to be placed on a bookshelf of anyone interested in the evolution of human settlement in Cambridgeshire from the Neolithic to the Anglo-Saxon age. The book, first published in 1923, was out of print for many years, but recently it has been made available as a digitally produced copy by Cambridge University Press. Dr Crowfoot went on to say that Cyril Fox once lived at 'Red Gables' (see illustration 106), unusually, for Milton, a red brick house, situated on the High Street next to the 'White Horse' public house opposite Butt Lane; the house was demolished many years ago to be replaced by modern houses. In memory of Cyril Fox's association with Milton, the cul-de-sac which is first on the right along Butt Lane, was named by the parish council as Fox's Close.

Dr Crowfoot continued. The few Mesolithic finds in Milton are confined to worked and burnt flints, and they have been found either side of Butt Lane towards the Mere Way, and on pasture land once belonging to Milton manor immediately to the east of the present day 18th century Milton Hall (work also carried out by OAE). However, Neolithic flints are more numerous and dispersed. The first, a single flake reported in Cyril Fox's book, was found south of Fen Road and more recently, another in a garden on the east side of the High Street. Other Neolithic flints, some defined as scrapers, have been found during fieldwalks and excavations on the Landfill Site, trench excavations behind Milton Hall and at the NAPP site in the Science Park (the latter work was carried out by Cambridge University Archaeological Unit). Both worked and burnt flints have been found at Hill Close and Long Meadow, fields to the north of Fen Road, but undated and could be of a later Bronze Age date. A late Neolithic pottery sherd (Peterborough ware) was found in excavations further northeast of Long Meadow.

Bronze Age

Dr Crowfoot continued further by saying, "Tom, we now move on in time from the 'lithic' or Stone Age peoples to those settlers who though still using flints, had progressed to making more substantial pottery, and for the first time started to use metal for tools and weapons. The first metal to be used was bronze (a mixture of copper and tin) giving rise to the Bronze Age (2,500 – 800 BC)." Tom replied, "Where have most of the Bronze Age finds been made in Milton?" Dr Crowfoot's answer was, "Again Tom, most of the Bronze Age artefacts including waterholes, pottery, post holes and evidence for 'round house' buildings, have been discovered during a series of excavations in fields on the Landfill Site during the 1990's and into the last decade. Of particular importance, are the finds for the Middle Bronze Age in Milton, they are of regional significance as very few sites have been excavated in Cambridgeshire, or indeed neighbouring counties. Bronze Age pottery has been found southeast of the A14/A10 interchange and in ditches and pits on land north of Fen Road just west of the railway line by Oxford Archaeology (the central organisation before the regional branch Oxford Archaeology East was established). Some of the flints found on the land behind Milton Hall could also have been Bronze Age. Our final evidence for Bronze Age people residing in Milton, arises from excavations carried out by the Cambridge University Archaeological Unit in the 1990's on land at the Cole's Road recreation ground destined for the building of the old peoples home, Barnabas Court. Here, Bronze Age pits and ditches were found, spanning the 2nd millenium BC, suggesting a more permanent occupation of the land at this time."

Iron Age

"Now Tom," exclaimed Dr Crowfoot, "we have reached that period in prehistory when significant and an increasing number of finds have been made in Milton, it is the Iron Age (800 BC – 43 AD)." Dr Crowfoot then continued to systematically review the sites and finds for this period in Milton's history.

The earliest record is reported by Cyril Fox for finds made when the sewage works were being established southeast of the parish at the beginning of the 20th century. The finds were good examples of Aylesford (Belgic) class, barrel urns – brick/red in colour.

Later, fieldwalking in fields in the north of the parish to the right of the Landbeach Road, produced a number of Iron Age pottery sherds. One late Iron Age silver coin of Tasciovanus of Catuvellauni (20BC-10AD), was found by metal detecting alongside the Mere Way north of Butt Lane. But, the largest number of finds have been made on the land destined to become the Landfill Site south of Butt Lane. This was a consequence of 'rescue' archaeology initiated by Dr Tim Reynolds as the Cambridgeshire County Archaeologist during the 1990's, and it led to a series of excavations yielding predominantly Iron Age and Roman material, as well as the earlier Neolithic and Bronze Age finds described earlier. Pottery, post holes, pits, hearths, beam slots, ditches, quarries and daub have been found across the site indicating significant Iron Age settlement. The fabric of the pottery was either 'gritty', tempered with white quartz or more rarely flint, or 'sandy' tempered with different grades of quartz sand. The colour was brown or reddish-brown, sometimes with a grey (reduced) core and the rims were decorated with fingertip impressions. To the west of this site towards the Mere Way at a later date, OAE found Iron Age waterholes and one with a log ladder. It seems occupation ceased in the early Roman period to be replaced by quarry working for high quality gravel, perhaps used to restore the Mere Way.

The alignment of the post holes suggested a number of functional features. For example, platforms constructed for drying grain or excarnation (exposure of cadavers to the weather and animals such as birds, before burial of the bones). Other patterns indicated Iron Age buildings by the finding of daub in the post holes. Still other alignments of double, parallel post holes suggested a fence.

Other Iron Age finds were a cremation and middens (waste pits) containing pottery. But, two particular finds from the Landfill Site were first, during a training excavation, a mid to late Iron Age cultivation feature consisting of 20 parallel ditches (0.6m wide, 0.3m deep and 2-3m apart) running northeast to southwest. These could have been 'lazy beds' acting as drainage ditches, but on which specific crops such as vines or asparagus might have been grown. Later work by the Cambridge University Archaeology Unit, extended excavations on this site and established the limits of the 'lazy beds'; they concluded that these features were Romano-British rather than Iron Age and were possibly linked to the earlier discovered Roman villa estate to the east of the site. Similar features have been found elsewhere including Bullocks Haste at Cottenham.

The second episode of Iron Age finds of note in Milton, was made at the old allotments site to the south of Butt Lane as rescue archaeology in 2006, before a new Park and Ride site was constructed. This site provided a considerable body of evidence for an Iron Age settlement with a complex of ditched enclosures, post holes for buildings, pits for rubbish including Iron Age pottery and bone, possible cremations and watering holes for use by humans and animals. These water holes contained mid to late Iron Age pottery and good wood preservation (due to anaerobic conditions in the water-logged state) exemplified as coppiced wood, a worked beam with mortised joints, and of notable interest, a log ladder radio - carbon dated to around 2500 BP.

On the eastern side of Milton, Iron Age pottery has been identified at the north end of the Country Park south of Old School Lane, and during fieldwalking at Hill Close off Fen Road, (organized by OAE supervising 6th form students). On the land behind Milton Hall and due north of Hill Close in excavations undertaken by OAE, 76 late Iron Age pottery sherds were identified together with post holes, pits, ditches and boundaries suggestive of an Iron Age settlement with agricultural activity (cereals, horses and cattle); these finds have been further substantiated more recently by Essex County Council Archaeologists. An Iron Age pit was found south of Fen Road and west of the railway on 1st terrace alluvium by Oxford Archaeology as part of a survey mentioned earlier when Bronze Age finds were made north of Fen Road; this was an archaeological evaluation of land to be used for the proposed Cambridge Rowing Course.

Dr Crowfoot concluded his tutorial on prehistoric Milton by saying, "Tom, at this early stage in our examination of Milton's archaeology, I hope you can see already that the finds show an increasing diversity in their nature, and that these reflect the lifestyle of the people of those far off days as they began to settle for longer periods of time in what is now our present day Milton parish – these early settlers were truly our first inhabitants."

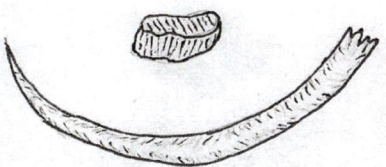

7. Stone Age: Mammoth tusk and tooth found south of Fen Road, Milton during gravel workings.
(diagrammatic representation)

8. Stone Age: Mesolithic/Neolithic flint scrapers found at Hill Close, Milton.

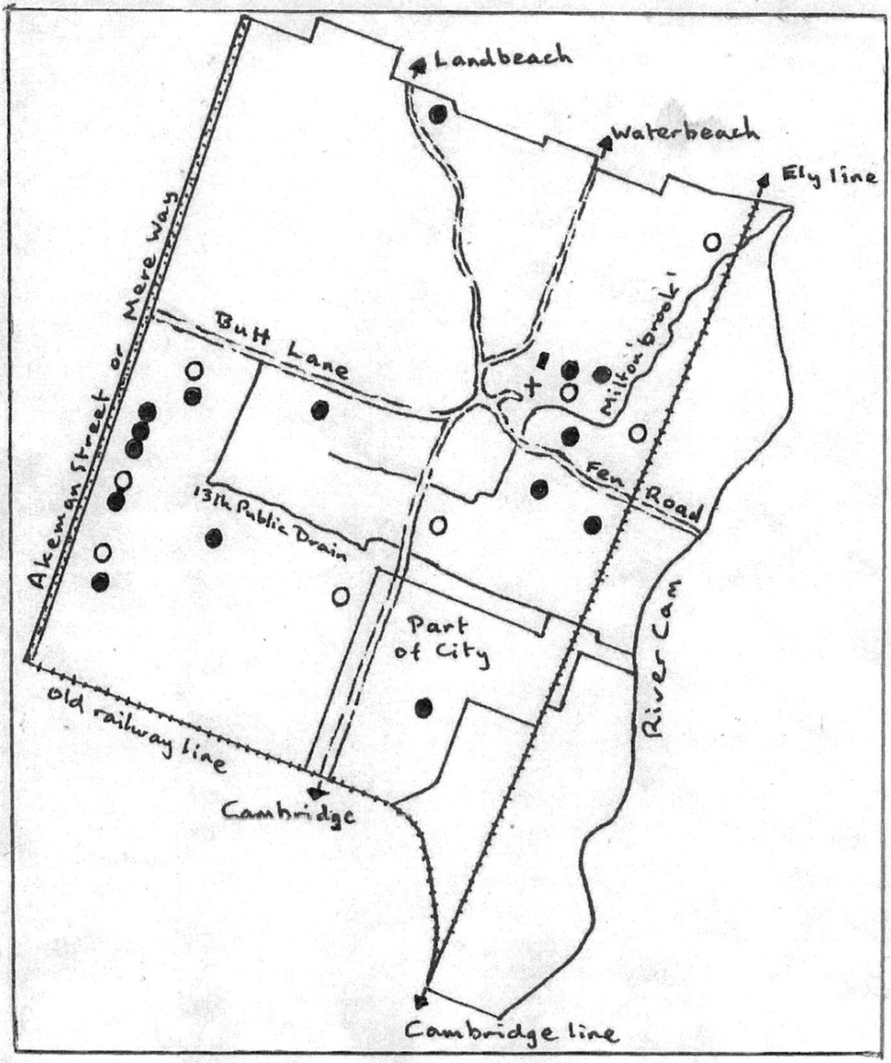

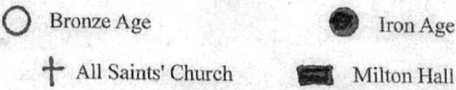

9. Bronze Age and Iron Age distribution of finds.

○ Bronze Age ● Iron Age
✝ All Saints' Church ▬ Milton Hall

10. Bronze Age: a typical collard urn.

11. Iron Age: Aylsford – Swarling (Belgic) urn. This type of urn was found by Sir Cyril Fox in the south part of Milton parish where the sewage works now exist.

3. Romans everywhere

Tom arrived at Kiln Cottage for his third Saturday morning tutorial with Dr Crowfoot. After consuming the usual refreshments prepared by Mrs Crowfoot, Dr Crowfoot then said to Tom, "Tom, this morning brings us to consider the most abundant archaeological artefacts found in Milton, they are those of the Roman period. But first, I will give you a brief outline of the Romans arriving in Britain.

A New Culture

"Although Julius Caesar as an important ruler in Rome, came to Britain in 55 and 54 BC, it was nearly 100 years later in 43 AD when the major invasion of Romans under the Emperor Claudius came to our shores, and the course of our history entered a new phase; this event is known as the Roman 'conquest' and resulted in the large impact the Romans had on our more simple Iron Age 'Celtic' lifestyle." Tom listened intently, this was going to be a very exciting morning's session. "A key factor about the Romans," Dr Crowfoot's commented, "was that they were very organised, and many well educated who could read and write in Latin – the dawn of history had arrived in Britain. In fact, before the Claudian invasion, Iron Age tribes had already been given Latin names and the tribal leaders went to Rome for an education; the Catuvellauni tribe was in the area of Milton, a tribe which extended northwest to the Midlands and southeast to London. The Roman society was supported by an efficient military force, which apart from conquering new lands, also initiated an infrastructure of roads and canals for communication conveying people as well as goods; "transportation is civilization" as quoted by Cyril Fox in his authoritative book.

The construction of substantial buildings known as villas built from stone, brick and with tiled roofs, were made for those in high authority i.e. at Fishbourne, West Sussex, while other development complexes, often with little masonry but of timber construction, were built as farming settlements. Kilns were established around Britain to produce more refined pottery than the Iron Age vessels, for the kitchen (course ware) and for the table (fine ware), and in different parts of the country, distinct regional wares were produced. Metal ores from different parts of Britain were smelted down for producing fine tools, jewellery and weapons, and the production of coins from gold, silver and copper alloys was prolific throughout the Roman empire. Finally Tom, the Iron Age farming methods were improved with the importation of new crops and animals leading to more sophisticated recipes for food. However, for many years the Iron Age culture, particularly farming methods were allowed to continue before the Roman and Iron Age systems eventually merged to give a hybrid culture, the 'Romano-British'."

Tom captivated by Dr Crowfoot's introduction to this new dynamic culture imposing itself on the fen-edge of what is now his village of Milton, was anxious to hear about the archaeological finds for the Romans in Milton. Dr Crowfoot then began his extensive review of the Roman artefacts discovered in the parish of Milton.

Roman roads

"Before I embark on a detailed review of Roman archaeology in Milton," Dr Crowfoot commented to Tom, as he sat more upright in his leather seated chair, with an aura of authority. " I will briefly return to last Saturday's tutorial when I referred to the boundaries of Milton parish. The relevance of the long, straight, west boundary separating the parishes of Milton and Impington, to today's session, is that it is in alignment with the Roman road we know as Akeman Street or Mere Way; I said previously that we would call the road the Mere Way in future reference to this road.

The Mere Way was a component of the cross-roads of Roman roads at Castle Hill in Cambridge where there was a small Roman town within a walled rectangular enclosure which may have been a military base guarding a river crossing over the River Cam at the foot of the hill; this was why the Roman town of Cambridge was called Durolipons - a substantial bridge. The town on the hill was on the site of an earlier Iron Age settlement.

The cross-roads were formed from the Mere Way running southwest to northeast, and the Via Devana running southeast to northwest from Colchester (Camulodunum) to Godmanchester (Durovigutum). The Mere Way ran north to Stretham, on to Ely, and possibly to the beginning of the higher land of west Norfolk near Denver; its course across the fens would have been dependent on small islands of gravel over clay emerging from the marsh land. An excavation at Milton revealed that the Mere Way was constructed of an agger (surface material) to a height of 0.45m, and was 10m wide, made up of hard-packed, clay-silt covered with 0.15m of compacted sand and gravel; either side of the road were flanking ditches up to 0.7m deep, and the dug out material from the ditches may have contributed to the road structure.

So here in Milton, Tom, we are privileged to have a stretch of Roman road that was probably an important transporting and communication route to the north of East Anglia from the Roman town of Cambridge and further south, as well as from the Milton area from which grain, animal products and pottery could have been conveyed. In this regard, Ken Humphries, a Milton resident with an interest in local history and archaeology, postulated a few decades ago that Butt Lane, a very straight road connecting with the Mere Way, in Roman times had a direct straight connection with Fen Road, equally more or less straight leading to the River Cam; this route constituted a secondary Roman road. The road would have been a useful connection between the Mere Way and the river for transport purposes." Dr Crowfoot said to Tom that this theory was a very plausible one which would become more obvious in the light of the finds he would describe shortly.

Water courses – Car Dyke

"But, there was another means of transportation in the area," Dr Crowfoot pronounced, and paused for a moment as he could see that Tom was trying to think what this might be, as expressed by a frown that looked as if it was going to lead to an answer in advance of his mentor's answer – Tom had to say it, " Was it the River Cam?" Dr Crowfoot with a positive smile said, "Yes Tom, you are partly right, like many rivers, they have been a major route for communication since the dawn of civilization, that is why so many important towns and cities have developed by rivers, London is a classical example. But, in our part of Cambridgeshire, the Romans were instrumental in extending our rivers with dug out channels sometimes connecting one river to another. For us it was the Car Dyke, dug out just outside our parish boundary with Waterbeach, in the latter half of the 2nd century AD, starting from the River Cam which was situated slightly to the west of its present course."

Dr Crowfoot continued to describe the significance of the Car Dyke to the Romans and its associated archaeology, with particular reference to Milton, but first the construction of the Car Dyke.

"Now Tom, why is the Car Dyke named as such? The Lincolnshire section of the dyke was known as Kari's Dyke in 1245, possibly after a Danish landowner called Karr, this would be in keeping with a word in the East Riding of Yorkshire for ditches, viz. Carr. However, whether Car or Carr, this could also mean a ditch in a landscape of marshland, reeds and shrubs with trees such as willow or alder. There have been differences of opinion with regard to the extent of the Car Dyke system, and therefore, its functional significance in the transportation of goods, particularly grain between our region of East Anglia to the north of England. The generally accepted view is that the Car Dyke connecting with the River Cam was dug out in a northwesterly direction to connect with the Old West branch of the River Ouse. From here via a complex of natural and excavated water courses, a section of the Car Dyke was constructed north of Ramsey to the River Nene at Peterborough – this was later called Cnut's Dyke. With reference to the Ordnance Survey map of Roman Britain, a distinct continuous water course ran north to connect with the River Witham at Lincoln (Lindum); this is known as the Lincolnshire Car Dyke. The River Witham was then connected to the River Trent by the Foss Dyke, and from here the River Trent connected directly with the River Humber, which in turn connected with the River Ouse to York (Eburacum). This was obviously a well thought out system, involving a considerable amount of labour to dig out a dyke up to 20m wide and 2.5m deep as seen at Waterbeach and Cottenham. But, it seems its use was over a relatively short time during the Roman occupation because there is evidence to suggest that the Car Dyke became filled in at the Waterbeach end by 280 AD, though seemly later at Bullock's Haste, Cottenham with a causeway constructed across the dyke by 375 AD. The Car Dyke at Waterbeach was eventually re-used in the 17th century for land drainage, and had become known as the Old Tillage or Twilade, a dialect word for loading and unloading.

An alternative view of the role of the Car Dyke system, is that even if there was a continuous waterway constructed from Waterbeach to Lincoln, some boats may have travelled along the rivers leading into the Wash viz. the Nene and the Ouse, then perhaps transferring goods to larger boats that went along the North Sea coast into the Humber and on to York. Some boats may have been destined to travel further to the northeast, or to the Rhine in Germany delivering grain."

Tom was captivated by the revelation of the extensive waterway system constructed by the Romans which enabled goods to be transported over 200km from essentially the south to the north of England avoiding the limits of road travel over hills and flooded valleys. But Tom did wonder how the Romans coped with the waterways during long periods of freezing conditions in winter, perhaps it was one reason why the Car Dyke was eventually abandoned – ice in our more northern climate was more frequent than in Rome? Another reason for abandonment might have been sabotage by local indigenous people infilling sections of the dyke? When Tom expressed his thoughts to Dr Crowfoot, Dr Crowfoot responded, " Tom, you raise some very practical aspects here, there is still plenty of scope for research on the advantages and limitations of the Car Dyke system. However, the general consensus of opinion is that the dyke went out of use due to unstable political and economic reasons, and rising sea levels, both factors making it difficult to maintain a patent waterway system, but still perhaps a drainage function. Now to the archaeology surrounding the Car Dyke nearer to home."

Car Dyke - archaeology

Dr Crowfoot began to summarize the archaeology that had been undertaken on the Car Dyke and its junction with the River Cam at Waterbeach. " During the last 20 years or so Tom, the County archaeologists as they were then, carried out excavations on the Car Dyke, and at its earlier connection with the River Cam just east of the railway track in fields overlying 1st terrace gravels and alluvium plain. The excavation suggested that there was a wide turning and docking area for river craft at the dyke-river junction, and that the area was a small 'port' with associated activities such as pottery production made in the kilns found on the site. The pottery associated with the kilns was local Horningsea grey ware, so called because a major source of this pottery was made in kilns on the other side of the River Cam on the site of Eye Hall farm at Horningsea. A distinctive type of Horningsea ware was the large wide storage jars with comb markings, suitable for storing and transporting grain or preserved meats – it would be these vessels that would be placed on the boats for transportation on the Car Dyke. The other type of Horningsea ware was the production of the grey course kitchen and table ware, we shall see later that this ware was also made in kilns at Milton.

Another find made at the Car Dyke junction, was evidence for a significant building, possibly a warehouse just north of the Milton parish boundary. The building with beam slots was contained in a 20m square plot and contained a considerable quantity of Horningsea grey ware, Nene Valley Colour Coated ware (NVCC) a fine table ware, and decorated Samian ware (terra sigillata) a high gloss - coated red ware, of high status from Gaul. If this pottery was not being stored in the warehouse for transportation along the Car Dyke, then it was probably being used locally for domestic purposes.

Other pottery found on the site, was some black burnished copies in Horningsea ware and 3rd to 4th century Nene Valley parchment mortaria used for grinding herbs etc.; all the pottery was wheel made. Several Roman coins were found on the site, essentially of low denomination made from a copper alloy, the highest value coins were dupondius and sesterstius dated to the Hadrianic, Antonine and Constantine periods. A cross disk, guilded brooch with a black-blue glass dated 2nd to 3rd century, was also found; a more utility find was a leather sandal."

Dr Crowfoot finished his account of the Car Dyke by referring to the section of the dyke at Bullock's Haste, Cottenham which had been excavated in the 1940's; a similar assemblage of pottery was found here to that found at the Car Dyke - River Cam junction. Bullock's Haste is the site of a significant Romano-British settlement and it is a scheduled ancient monument, as are 10 sections of the Car Dyke including that at Waterbeach on the west side of the railway track. Dr Crowfoot then quoted the conclusion of Stephen Macaulay who was the project leader for County archaeologists involved in the Car Dyke excavations, " the area north of Cambridge close to Milton, Landbeach, Horningsea and Waterbeach contains some of the most concentrated Roman archaeology in Cambridgeshire" - this would become more apparent by the time Dr Crowfoot had dealt with the Romans at Milton.

South of the Car dyke

At this stage in the morning's tutorial, Dr Crowfoot had dealt with communication routes in and out of the Milton area under the Roman occupation, and had begun to reveal some of the artefacts, notably pottery which had been found near the Car Dyke. This site was a convenient location to move from, south into the present day parish of Milton and review Roman artefacts found in different locations in the parish, and in some cases associated with good evidence for Romano-British settlements.

Dr Crowfoot reshuffled his notes together and folded his Ordnance Survey map to focus on Milton so that he could point out to Tom the various locations where Roman finds had been made in the village. "Now Tom," Dr Crowfoot uttered, "brace yourself for much data and the significance of its location." Dr Crowfoot then commenced his long account, looking at the map, and concentrating on the land west of the River Cam, and particularly west of the railway track before the A10 to Waterbeach – the richest area for Roman finds in Milton. There has been a succession of excavations carried out along the 1st and 2nd terrace deposits running in a southwest to northeast alignment from Fen Road north to the Car Dyke; some of the excavations and fieldwalking have been carried out because of the pending threat of much of the land being destined for the Cambridge Rowing Lake, a proposal under review since 1992, but as yet this has not materialized.

A significant feature about the finds, is that they have occurred in a corridor primarily on the 2nd terrace deposits. Whether fieldwalks or excavations, the pottery types found were similar to those described for the Car Dyke excavations i.e. Horningsea grey wares, NVCC, Samian and mortaria, with a few sherds from other sources such as Hadham. Two kiln sites were discovered, one in the north of the area, the other further south; both sites were producing Horningsea grey wares. In addition to many bones from large domestic farm animals, two Romano-British

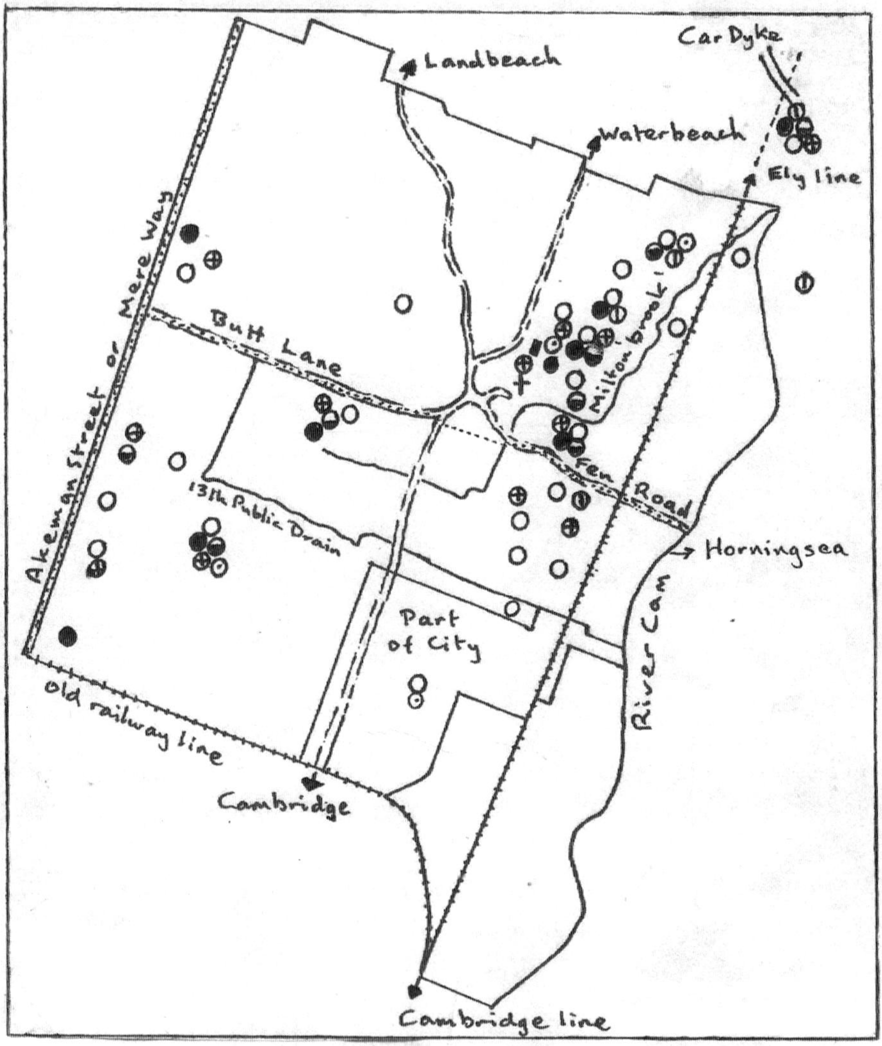

12. Romano-British distribution of finds.

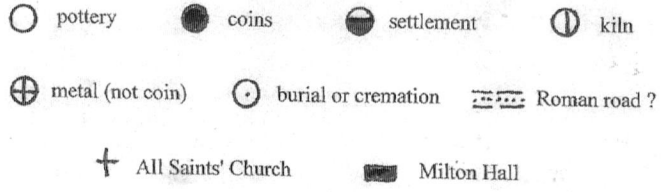

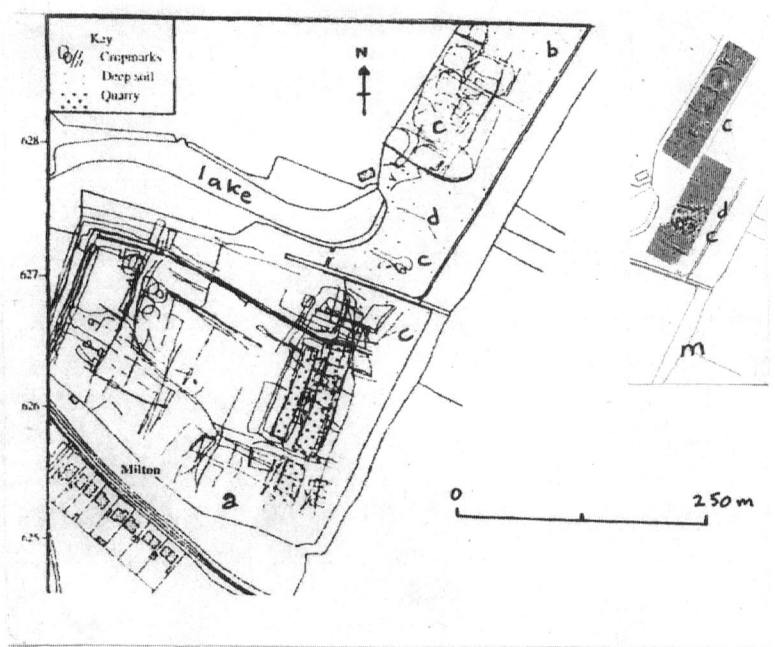

13. Romano-British activity at Hill Close and Long Meadow, Milton as revealed by crop marks. (after Palmer in Robinson & Guttman, 1996), and magnetometry (m): © Ian Sanderson of Archaeology Rheesearch, 2008.

(a) Hill Close (b) Long Meadow (c) Romano-British farmstead settlement

(d) earlier course of Milton brook

inhumation cemeteries were discovered at the most northern kiln site. At the southern kiln site, four Roman coins were found including two of Gallic emperors (254 - 276 AD), one falling off a horse (Constantius II 345-362 AD) and one small minim. This latter site was excavated by the Reverend Professor W H C Frend, otherwise known as 'Bill' Frend (a scholar of early Christianity and an archaeologist), with the help of the voluntary Cambridge Archaeological Field Group. Incidentally, to the east of the railway track, in a small field before a bend in the River Cam, Derek Booth the Milton Archaeological Warden, found in the 1980's several black burnished sherds of Horningsea grey ware, in clumps on the surface of the field, suggesting dredging deposits from the river, which at this point was near the Roman pottery kilns at Horningsea.

Romans in northeast Milton

Progressing further south along the 2nd terrace deposits to Long Meadow east of Milton Hall, brings us to a highly productive site for Romano-British finds found through fieldwalking in 2006 and 2007, and a few test pits dug in 2008. A systematic fieldwalk was carried out on recently ploughed and wheat sown soil at Long Meadow, by 6th form students from the Perse and Hills Road 6th Form Colleges under the supervision of the then County archaeologists; the initiator of the investigation was Derek Booth. Over 25kg of the usual distinctive pottery for a Romano-British site in the area, was retrieved, ranging from Horningsea grey wares, to Samian and mortaria, and two pieces of Roman light blue pillar-moulded glass from a bowl. There were also a number of pudding stone (nature's 'concrete' – pebbles embedded in clay/chalk from Hertfordshire) quernstones, and gritsand grindstone fragments were present. Other finds were fragments of tiles and a number of oyster shells. Of particular note, was the relatively large number (over 40) of low denomination copper alloy Roman coins, ranging from the 1st to 4th centuries. Two of the coins are worthy of comment, they were Constantine (330-335 AD), the first Christian emperor; one showed the reverse with a wolf suckling twins Romulus and Remus (urbs issue), the other the reverse showed soldiers with a standard. Other metal objects found by voluntary metal detectorists, for the Roman period, were parts of two copper alloy Colchester brooches, a possible copper alloy bracelet and a silver ring. Test pits dug across ditch features in 2008, by Derek Booth with the assistance of Active 8 Archaeology, provided more comparable Roman pottery.

With Dr Crowfoot having bombarded Tom with a vast array of Romano-British finds made at Long Meadow, what did all this data mean? Once again, Tom had that puzzled look, his brain was beginning to click into action to hopefully pose an intelligent question to Dr Crowfoot, which he did, "Dr Crowfoot, were there any 'hot spots' for the distribution of the finds in Long Meadow, if so, could they indicate that perhaps there was a settlement here?" Dr Crowfoot with a confident smile, replied without hesitation, "Tom, already you have the makings of an archaeologist, your question is right on the mark! Yes, the majority of the finds were concentrated at the west side of this rectangular field within a 120m x 50m area on the highest land which was above 5m OD. Furthermore, earlier crop marks revealed by aerial photography, and magnetometry carried out before the fieldwalks, showed a coincidence of the crop marks with the magnetometry. These data revealed a ladder development of approximately 20m square enclosures running southwest to northeast, with a possible track between the enclosures, and the whole surrounded by an enclosure feature, suggestive of a ditch – all these data together suggested the presence of a relatively high status Romano-British farmstead settlement. The main products of the farmstead were likely to have been grain, with some processing to flour as indicated by the quernstones, and animals, as the majority of bone and teeth from large farm animals such as horse, cattle, sheep and pig were predominant on the proposed settlement site. There was also a similar bias for oyster shells, building materials and natural stone being concentrated at the west side of Long Meadow, providing further data to support the presence of a significant settlement."

But this was only part of the story for Long Meadow. Dr Crowfoot continued, "Tom, the aerial photography and coincident magnetometry showed features at the south end of Long Meadow quite separate from the main settlement on the west side of the field. Furthermore, there was a line feature across the field at its lowest level which often had lying water present after rain. What did these features mean? The fieldwalk at the southern end of the field resulted in large amounts of pottery and quernstone fragments being retrieved; a significant amount of the pottery was Horningsea storage vessel sherds. A later test pit in 2008 at the centre of the site revealed charcoal and iron deposits. Therefore, the finds at this southern end of the field suggested this was an industrial area associated with processing grain, and that the feature at the lowest point in the field, was the original stream course of the Milton brook. This was later in the 18th century, dammed up to form the boating lake nearby in Milton Hall grounds as part of the 'natural' landscaping carried out by Humphrey Repton. The Milton brook in Roman times would have had more water flowing through it, enough to provide the main settlement and the 'industrial' site as one working complex. (Incidentally, with the old water course being dammed up to form the lake, the water was directed from the east end of the lake as over - spill, through a south directed conduit before turning east in a ditch between Long Meadow and Hill Close). A general conclusion to be drawn from all the data for Long Meadow, is that there was a significant native homestead here associated with agricultural, proto-industrial activity supplying grain and possibly flour to be transported north via the Car Dyke about 1km away, or south along the River Cam to Cambridge."

Dr Crowfoot had one more piece of archaeological data to widen the perspective of the settlement in Long Meadow. "Tom, in the field immediately to the west of Long Meadow and before Milton Hall, the OAE archaeologists in 2008 dug several trenches on this one time training ground for electricians working for EDF; the archaeology was carried out in advance of a proposed residential development. The trenches revealed several Iron Age ditches and pits as I informed you in our last tutorial on the prehistoric period. But in addition, Roman pottery was found on the site and of particular interest, a 2nd to 3rd century cremation of a young adult with the remains placed in an urn; in the same trench, was recovered a 1st century Rosette brooch, a copper alloy ring and a 3rd century bone pin. This trench was only a few metres from the settlement at Long Meadow, separated by a small dry ditch and a barbed wire fence. One wonders if this is a very ancient field boundary back to Roman times with perhaps a small cemetery just west of Long Meadow in the vicinity of the cremation remains that were found. A few low denomination Roman coins of the 3rd to 4th century were also found on the EDF site. Incidentally, a Roman fibula brooch had been discovered earlier in the grounds near Milton Hall. Most of the Roman pottery was found at the eastern end of the EDF site nearest Long Meadow, consisting of both coarse and fine wares as found at Long Meadow. Subsequent excavations in 2013 by Essex County Council archaeologists found similar results which suggests that the Roman activity at the eastern end of the EDF field and at Long Meadow are the same Romano-British settlement.

By now, Tom was getting really excited by all these Roman finds in his village, how many more might there be? Tom was soon to realize that this was only the beginning. Dr Crowfoot picked up the map again and said to Tom, "We will now take a look at the large square field adjacent to and south of Long Meadow, it is known as Hall End or Hill Close. Here in 2007, a second fieldwalk was carried out by the same two Cambridge 6th form colleges that were involved in the previous fieldwalk at Long

Meadow, and also the same metal detectorists were involved. Earlier aerial photography, had revealed a large number of crop marks at Hill Close, indicating marked ditch features at the west end of the field forming a 'moat' around the site of a supposed manor house; this will be the subject of a later tutorial. At the northeast corner of Hill Close was another complex of linear crop marks, and it was here that the fieldwalk recovered the largest amount of Roman pottery in the ploughed field, primarily sherds of the large Horningsea vessels, and the metal detectorists found over 25 Roman copper alloy coins ranging from the 1st to the 4th century; these were confined mostly to the northeast corner of the field. Two coins are worthy of note: a single 1st to 2nd century As or dupondius and a 4th century coin of the Arles mint, pierced as a possible re-use in the early Anglo-Saxon period; a test pit here in 2008 revealed more Roman pottery and a few more Roman coins. Other Roman finds at Hill Close were a pin head, a pot mend, part of a bone dice and part of a Colchester brooch. Due to the close proximity of this site to the south end of Long Meadow with its suggested industrial site, it is likely that both sites formed one industrial complex and the relatively large number of coins found may reflect a focus for trading."

Romans in Milton Country Park

Dr Crowfoot then said to Tom, "We have dealt with the major Roman archaeology on the north side of Milton, next we will consider some earlier finds made when the gravel pits were being excavated between 1930 and 1960 south of Fen Road, the area is now part of Milton Country Park. I think a good way of appreciating the wide distribution of Roman finds in the country park," Dr Crowfoot exclaimed, "is to take an imaginary walk round the park, starting at the entrance from Fen Road. On entering the park in the area where the mammoth tusk and tooth were found as mentioned in last week's tutorial, Roman pottery was also discovered during gravel excavations. Walking further into the park and looking across the overgrown wetlands area to the eastern extremity of the park towards the railway and close to Fen Road, here was found a Roman pottery kiln, then further south on the 1st terrace deposits, a Roman iron knife was discovered under a calf's skull in a pit. Further still into the park on the eastern side of Dickerson's pit, was found more Roman pottery and another kiln. Ken Humphries the local historian reported on pottery kilns and pottery found during gravel excavations in the park, commenting that Milton was also producing a form of Horningsea grey ware.

Continuing across the wooden bridge over the 13th public drain, brings us to the D-Day Remembrance Meadows and the site of the recovery of more Roman pottery. This area was once part of the sewage works complex, now intercepted by the A14. At the sewage works on the Cambridge side of the A14, when the sewage works were being established in 1903, Cyril Fox reports the finding of Roman pottery which was predominantly Horningsea grey ware, with a minimum of fine wares including Samian. This together with some Belgic pottery, and some human and animal bones suggested a farmstead settlement, again another Roman settlement like that at Long Meadow on 2nd terrace deposits not far from the flood plain of the River Cam." Dr Crowfoot was keen to point out to Tom the parallels in sites of occupation by the Romano-British people, he continued.

"Let us in our imaginary walk return to the main part of the country park by crossing the large wooden bridge back over the 13th public drain between Hall's Pool and Dickerson's pit. Close to the west bank of Dickerson's pit, near the jetty, further Roman pottery sherds were found during gravel extraction. Finally, we leave the north part of the park at the Old School Lane entrance, but near the exit, Roman pottery and beads were found, while just outside the park an intriguing coloured, lead figurine of a Roman emperor was discovered."

Romans in west Milton

Dr Crowfoot then said to Tom, "We are now nearing the end of this week's intensive tutorial on Roman Milton, the last areas we have got to look at are north and south of Butt Lane. First to the north of Butt Lane, in fields just to the west of Rectory Farm, here an assemblage of Roman pottery was found, but not in any particular context. However, close to the Mere Way, north of Butt Lane, a wide selection of Roman pottery sherds were identified including, grey wares, NVCC and Samian wares. Furthermore, in the same area, metal detecting recovered some 3rd century Roman copper alloy coins including three Constantine radiates, four barbarous radiates (cheap copies) and a radiate of Constantine III. Other Roman metal finds, were a bronze finger ring, two bronze bow brooches and a bronze jug handle. This array of Roman finds is what metal detectorists are looking for near Roman roads, but whether the cluster of finds to the east of the Mere Way is related to a particular focus of activity here, is unknown.

However, across Butt Lane to the south, we are back to the Landfill Site again." Dr Crowfoot reminded Tom of the prehistoric finds made here. "Again Tom, the County archaeologists have been responsible for Roman finds during a number of excavations on this large area of land. Here, excavations near the Mere Way in the southwest corner of the parish produced several 1st to 4th century pottery sherds and a hair pin. Quarry pits on the site may have been associated with the construction of the Mere Way. Moving east towards the source of the 13th public drain, more Roman pottery sherds were found. But, the major Roman excavation here, just south of the drain was that carried out under the supervision of the County archaeologist Dr Tim Reynolds during the 1990's. Tim's team revealed a Roman villa estate with many ditches, large amounts of pottery, two Colchester type fibula, 3rd to 4th century coins, a 1st to 2nd century glass bottle, Roman roof and box tiles, timber barns, corn drier, a smithy, cattle trough, a cemetery around a low mound containing

19 inhumations (3rd to 4th century) and three 2nd century cremations. Associated with the burials were two small wine flagons, each pierced with a small hole (presumably to make them unusable in the 'after life'), and in one burial a NVCC cup was at the feet, while another burial had a bone comb. All these finds indicated that a high status settlement had developed here, perhaps an area authority for the agricultural industry including the settlements along the River Cam terraces i.e. from the present sewage works, Long Meadow to the Car Dyke? It is of interest that outside the southern boundary of Milton parish at Arbury, an even more impressive villa site had been excavated earlier."

"Tom," Dr Crowfoot uttered with a relieved expression, "one last small piece of evidence for the Romans in Milton. During the excavation south of Butt Lane nearest the village on the site destined to become the new Park and Ride terminus at Milton, as mentioned in my last tutorial, evidence for a significant Iron Age settlement was found here. But, as is so often the case when the Iron Age peoples found a desirable place to live, the Romans followed with their influence on the same site – this was the case with the Park and Ride site. Superimposed on the Iron Age features at the eastern end of the site, was evidence for a Roman enclosure ditch with its associated pottery, the Romans may have arrived here 300 years after the development of the Iron Age settlement.

So Tom, we have now finished our marathon tutorial on the Romans at Milton. In summary, the extent of the Roman finds in and close to the village is considerable, the finds being made at random and by planned fieldwalks and excavations. Although a grand villa constructed of brick and stone with mosaic floors has yet to be found in Milton, we do have the legacy of a Roman road, the Mere Way which today is a grassy track between hedgerows of blackthorn, hawthorn, shrubs and wild flowers conserving nature for our appreciation as we walk north towards Landbeach. If we meander south along the Mere Way in the direction of Cambridge, the track is bordered by large trees at its southern end. There is also a good section of the nationally significant Car Dyke, not many metres from our northern parish boundary with Waterbeach – the Romans truly made an impact on our landcape for a few hundred years until they left our shores around 410 AD.

But, before we finally finish this tutorial, I want to illustrate with reference to an artefact found at the Romano-British site, Long Meadow, during the fieldwalking, that even professional archaeologists sometimes find it difficult to identify a find. The artefact in question, was initially identified as a 2nd century Roman disc brooch in keeping with the context of the site. However, an authority involved with the Portable Antiquities Scheme, disagreed with the identification and concluded that it was an 18th century copy, fashionable as women's jewellery at this time. But, what a coincidence that the brooch was found on a Romano-British site! Perhaps it had been worn by one of the ladies at Milton Hall nearby?

In our next tutorial, we will take a look at what followed the Romans – it was the 'Dark Ages' when our civilization partly went backwards in time, but also moved forward with a more lasting effect on our village than that provided by the Romans."

14. Horningsea storage jars: left, rim; right body, found at Long Meadow, Milton.

15. Coarse sandy grey ware found at Long Meadow, Milton.

16. Oxidised course ware found at Long Meadow, Milton.

17. Top left, sandy grey ware base; top right, goblet base; bottom left and right, 'foot rings' goblet bases found at Long Meadow, Milton.

18. Nene Valley Colour Coated ware (NVCC) found at Long Meadow, Milton.

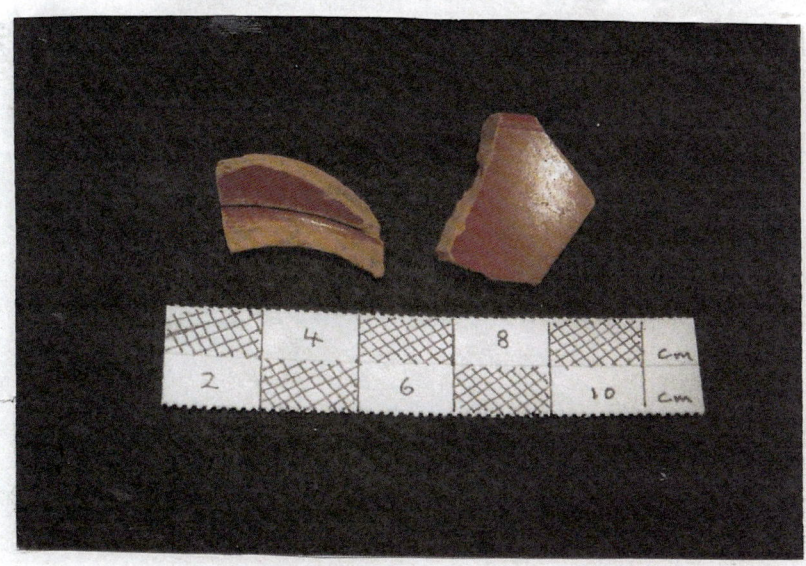

19. Plain Samian ware found at Long Meadow, Milton.

20. Mortaria for grinding herbs: left, rim; right, base found at Long Meadow, Milton.

21. Flagons found with a Roman cremation (2nd century) at the Landfill Site.
© Alison Taylor

22. Excavating a Roman cremation urn at the Landfill Site.
© Alison Taylor

23. 2nd - 3rd century cremation at the earlier EDF site (rear of Milton Hall).

24. Pudding stone: part of a quern stone found at Long Meadow, Milton.

25. Grit stone: use as a grindstone, note sharpening grooves, Long Meadow, Milton.

26. Part of Roman roof tile *(tegula)*, Long Meadow, Milton.

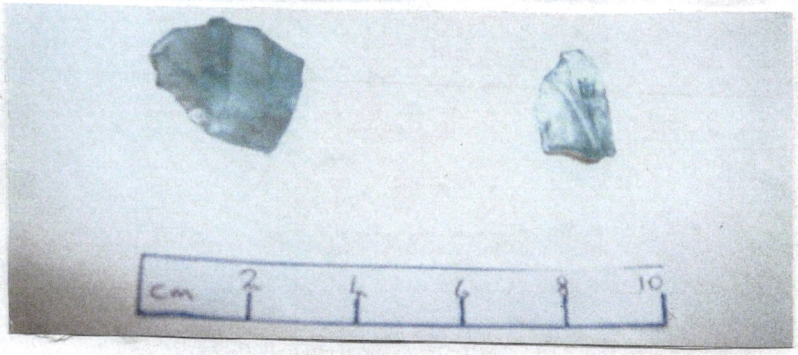

27. Glass fragments of Romano-British pillar-moulded bowl, Long Meadow, Milton.

28. Coin of the Emperor Julian II, 'The Apostate' (AD 360-363), Landfill Site.
© Alison Taylor

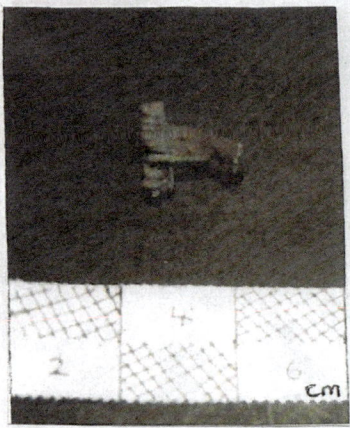

29. Part of a Colchester (sprung pin) bow brooch, Long Meadow, Milton.

30. The Roman Road – the Mere Way at Milton looking south towards Butt Lane.

4. Anglo-Saxons - founders of Milton

Another Saturday morning had arrived, but not an inspiring one – it was autumn, the clouds were leaden and threatening rain, and the wind was gathering strength from the east; all Tom wanted to do was to creep further under the sheets. But, his curiosity got the better of him, he glanced at the alarm clock on the small table beside his bed – it was 8.00 am; no more lingering in bed, Tom had to wash, put on presentable clothes and grab some breakfast before setting off on his bicycle for his fourth tutorial with Dr Crowfoot by 9.00 am; already a month had gone by since his first tutorial.

As Tom cycled from his house into the High Street and round the corner into Fen Road, the east wind blasted a cascade of large stinging rain drops into his face, Tom, suddenly, was reminded of the saying, "when the wind blows from the east, 'tis neither good for man or beast", therefore what better place to be than sitting in front of Dr Crowfoot's log fire with a warming cup of coffee and a freshly cooked, crunchy, home-made biscuit – cocooned from the elements, if only for an hour, and learning about the origins of his village Milton, in Anglo-Saxon times.

When Tom arrived at the gate of Kiln Cottage, he could see Caesar the Siamese cat pacing up and down before the front door, waiting to be let into the comforts of the cottage which would assist in drying out his wet fur. What a relief for Caesar to see Tom giving the usual three knocks on the solid door. Within moments, Dr Crowfoot greeted the two bedraggled beings who entered the refuge, Caesar for his fishy breakfast in the kitchen, and Tom for his reviving coffee snack and another inspiring tutorial to feed his mind.

Saxons arrive

"This morning Tom," Dr Crowfoot exclaimed in a relaxed manner, as both he and Tom sat down in their usual chairs either side of the fire place with its glowing fire, "we will consider what life was like for those inhabitants in the Milton area after the Romans had retreated back to Rome, their vast empire collapsing due to it being overstretched and unable to defend itself against marauding peoples from the east. But, this did not suddenly happen in Britain, the Romans had been trading with the Germanic peoples on the continent of Europe well before the collapse of their empire at the beginning of the 5th century; the main Germanic group involved with sea trade, was the Anglo-Saxons. Therefore, when the Roman influence finally left Britain, their forts on the 'Saxon Shore' of the east and southeast coasts of England, were abandoned, and their function as a defence against unwanted Saxon pirates was lost. The consequence of this was that the Anglo-Saxons arrived on our shores unchallenged, and introduced a new culture and a new phase in our history. Initially, there was the suppression of the Christian religion introduced to the earlier Romano-British culture by Constantine I in the 4th century, and a return of our life style to a more primitive culture – this was the beginning of the 'Dark Ages', and they were to last for the next 500 years or so, until the Norman invasion of 1066."

Dr Crowfoot wanted Tom to imagine what Milton might have been like after the last Roman authority had left the area and the Anglo-Saxons had arrived. Dr Crowfoot then endeavoured to help Tom to illuminate his imagination by recalling the Roman landscape waiting to be changed by the Anglo-Saxons.

"The Anglo-Saxons," Dr Crowfoot exclaimed, "Would have been migrating inland from the east and south coasts of England after their journey across the North Sea from present day north Germany. They would have used the infrastructure of Roman roads as well as the natural water courses of the larger rivers, moving up river from the estuaries. With reference to Milton, primary road routes to our area from the east would have been the Via Devana from Colchester to Cambridge, and from the south along Ermine Street from London, then a northeast, secondary Roman road leading off Ermine Street near present day Wimpole, to Cambridge. From Cambridge, the Mere Way would still have been a major route to the Milton area. Alternative approaches would have been across East Anglia via a number of trackways including the ancient Icknield Way, and possibly down the Rivers Ouse and Cam from the Wash, a route taken by those Anglo-Saxons arriving on the north coast of Norfolk, or the Lincolnshire coast.

What scene would have met the eyes of the first Anglo-Saxons as they approached the Milton area? Approaching from the Mere Way, the landscape would have been dotted with Romano-British farmsteads of different sizes together with industrial sites producing pottery, tiles, metal tools, building materials (mostly wood) and domestic products. If the Anglo-Saxons had come south from the Wash, as soon as they arrived in the vicinity of present day Waterbeach, they would have seen an almost continuous development of Romano-British farmstead settlements some now showing signs of neglect, running south to Cambridge along a ridge of slightly higher land to the west, and to the east on even higher land, the remnants of the Roman pottery works at Horningsea. Between the farmsteads with their open land for crops and for grazing farm animals, there would have been more extensive woodland than seen today."

Dr Crowfoot continued, "One wonders what the reaction of the local British people was (then presumably they were still living in the settlements established by the Romans), to the Anglo-Saxons entering their area in increasing numbers. There certainly was armed resistance, but eventually an acceptance of the new immigrants because they were not too different in their origins. Five hundred years earlier, the British as late Iron Age people, had been exposed to the Roman culture, but as Celts, their roots were similar to the Celts of northern Europe i.e. the Anglo-Saxons.

Perhaps also, our people were relieved that the Roman authority had gone, and together with the Anglo-Saxons they could lead a less pressurised life style. This view seems to be supported by the fact that the indigenous British people did not retain the more sophisticated culture brought to them by the Romans other than Christianity, and so they happily returned to a more simple life style which they and the Anglo-Saxons had in common. Notable common characteristics of both British and Anglo-Saxon cultures, were the domestic dwellings which were simple wooden structures with thatched roofs. The early Anglo-Saxon pottery was relatively crude not unlike the pottery of the late Iron Age people in Britain which the post Roman British were happy to return to.

Although we do not know how long the post Roman British stayed in their Romano-British settlements, we do know that the Anglo-Saxons did not like constructing their settlements directly on the Roman sites (unless they were military forts i.e. Castle Hill, Cambridge) – perhaps this was in part superstition, the early Anglo-Saxons were pagan, the later Romano-British were Christian since the conversion of the Roman emperor Constantine I to Christianity in the early 4th century. In due course, the post Roman British and Anglo-Saxon cultures merged and new settlements were established, but not necessarily too far from the earlier Romano-British sites; this is suggested by the limited Anglo-Saxon finds we have in Milton."

Dr Crowfoot paused for a moment to collect his thoughts while he and Tom drank the last of the nearly cold coffee. Dr Crowfoot then rose from his chair and selected a large log from the basket next to the fireplace and placed it on the substantial bed of glowing embers which had built up in the grate – this piece of well-seasoned timber would maintain the welcoming heat in the room for the remainder of the tutorial.

Evidence for Saxon settlement

The short break of necessary activity refreshed both tutor and student before Dr Crowfoot continued with the tutorial, "Unlike some other villages in Cambridgeshire Tom, significant evidence for Anglo-Saxon presence including a cemetery, particularly of the pagan period with its associated grave goods, has unfortunately not yet been discovered in Milton. However, like our neighbouring villages Histon, Impington, Girton and Oakington (the latter two villages with significant Anglo-Saxon finds including burials), Milton is one of the 'ton' villages - an Anglo-Saxon 'town' settlement. The Anglo-Saxon name for Milton was 'Middeltun' – a middle place, perhaps between the dryer land around the Mere Way to the west, and the marsh land by the River Cam to the east. After the Anglo-Saxon period, there were further changes to the name of the village after the Norman Conquest which eventually gave rise to the present name of Milton, but these will be dealt with in our next tutorial".

At this point in the tutorial, Tom once again looked puzzled – he could not understand why no evidence for Anglo-Saxon dwellings or burials had yet been found in Milton when it was an Anglo-Saxon foundation, the more so since there has been so much housing development in the village, including his parents house; surely one would have expected some Anglo-Saxon material to have been exposed? These thoughts, Tom put to Dr Crowfoot who replied with a degree of hesitation, "Tom, you are right, it does seem a little extraordinary that with so much of the land in Milton parish particularly near the centre of the present village having been turned over by the plough for farming, or the excavator for building foundations over centuries, nothing of a convincing Anglo-Saxon settlement has been recorded. However, let us consider what evidence we have got which suggests Anglo-Saxon settlement in, or near our village".

Dr Crowfoot continued, "although no Anglo-Saxon cemetery has been found near the centre of Milton village, a few Anglo-

Saxon burials were found while excavating for gravel in the extreme southeast corner of the parish near the railway line on land that was once part of the parish of Chesterton. Similarly, with reference to the archaeology around the Roman Car Dyke at Waterbeach, Tom, we have again to go just outside our parish to Waterbeach to find the Anglo-Saxons. At two sites in Waterbeach to the west of and near to the Car Dyke, simple Anglo-Saxon hut buildings (10' x 8') with sunken floors were found during excavations by a well-known Cambridge archaeologist, Tom Lethbridge over 80 years ago; these early Anglo-Saxon buildings are called 'grubenhauser' (plural) or 'grubenhaus' (single). Associated with these dwellings were found parts of two swords, a shield boss, spear and human skulls, a gilded pendant or brooch, hand thrown decorated pottery, red beads, yellow and green glass, bone and bronze needles, three spindle – whorls, a perforated boar's tusk and fragments of distinctive ivory bag rings; near the site was a suggestive cemetery. The nature of the finds indicated early Anglo-Saxon settlement which occurred between the 5th and 7th centuries AD, an essentially pagan period".

Saxons in Milton

"Now Tom, we come south back into the parish of Milton to review the significance of the very limited Anglo-Saxon material which has been found here. There is circumstantial evidence to suggest that the site of All Saints' Church was an Anglo-Saxon foundation before the Norman Conquest in 1066. As no masonry, of this period has been recorded during restoration and expansion of the post Norman church during past centuries, it is concluded that any church built on the site before 1066 was likely to have been a timber structure. Evidence from other parish church sites has shown that Anglo-Saxon timber built churches were erected before the post Norman buildings, but little remained of the timber since the excavation of the soil and placing substantial post Norman foundations, would have masked or obliterated most of the evidence. However, before 1066, Milton would have been under the bishopric of Ely where a monastery was founded in 673 AD by the East Anglian princess Etheldreda".

Dr Crowfoot continued, "Tom, on the assumption Milton had an Anglo-Saxon church on the site of our present All Saints' Church, this implies that there was likely to have been an Anglo-Saxon settlement nearby – the first focus of inhabitants to establish the village of Milton. Now we do have that little bit of Anglo-Saxon archaeology, to support not only the presence of Anglo-Saxons in Milton with the random find of an Anglo-Saxon bronze wrist clasp at the Landfill Site off Butt Lane, but more significantly 'nearer to home' and only 200m from All Saints' Church, some more significant Anglo-Saxon finds have been made.

During the fieldwalking of Hill Close off Fen Road during 2007 by students from Cambridge sixth form colleges supervised by professional archaeologists, and also involving voluntary metal detectorists and our parish archaeological warden Derek Booth as mentioned in our last tutorial, the following finds were made at the west end of the field. With regard to pottery, two sherds of high status Ipswich ware (650-850 AD)were found together with one St Neot's ware sherd (850-1150 AD) and two Thetford ware sherds (900-1200 AD). Furthermore, to substantiate the Anglo-Saxon context, metal detectorists found part of an Anglo-Saxon copper alloy tweezer and a Roman 4th century copper alloy coin of the Arles mint with a pierced hole for probable re-use in an early Anglo-Saxon necklace; the Anglo-Saxons had no use for Roman coins as currency as they tended to trade by exchanging goods. So here at last Tom, we have a 'hot spot' for albeit just a few Anglo-Saxon artefacts in Milton; the nearest other Anglo-Saxon find was a 6-7th century AD copper alloy pin head found during the student fieldwalking project on the adjacent field, Long Meadow during 2006. The 'hot spot' for Anglo-Saxon finds ranging from the early Anglo-Saxon period (the pierced Roman coin) to the late Anglo-Saxon period (the pottery) at Hill Close, is the first archaeological evidence for a focal presence of Anglo-Saxons in Milton. Of particular interest, is the relatively close proximity of Hill Close to the parish church and its likely Anglo-Saxon origins, and the fact that an anecdote passed down through the ages to the present day that Hill Close is locally referred to as 'the village'. How true this seems to be with some archaeology to substantiate the origins of Anglo-Saxon settlement at Milton, established in a typical location, a short distance away from an earlier Romano-British settlement at Long Meadow".

Milton favourable to the Saxons

Having dealt with finds indicating an Anglo-Saxon settlement off Fen Road, Dr Crowfoot then proceeded to consider some other factors which favour a continuing settlement by invaders to the area. "You recall Tom", Dr Crowfoot continued, "that the prehistoric peoples and the Romans found the Milton landscape highly suitable for settlement. Likewise, so did the Anglo-Saxons. There was a natural water course, the Milton brook, running through the land of past settlements, and an infrastructure of roads with the Mere Way linked via Butt Lane and Fen Road to the River Cam as likely to have been established by the Romans. As the Anglo-Saxons generally preferred to establish their settlements away from earlier Roman settlements unless they had strategic defensive attributes, the area to the north of Fen Road and slightly to the west with a cap of higher land, became the suitable site for building the first church – this allowed for settlement between the church and the Roman activity at the eastern end of Hill Close and at Long Meadow. Furthermore, the Anglo-Saxons were quite happy with narrow tracks with bends, therefore the present Church Lane may well have been an original Anglo-Saxon access road as Anglo-Saxon settlement spread westwards towards the centre of our present day village with its High Street.

Finally, another feature which may have an Anglo-Saxon origin, or even earlier back to the Iron Age, is the so-called moat at the west end of Hill Close just beyond the Anglo-Saxon finds, which has been assumed to be part of the moat system surrounding the 13th century manor house, to be considered in the next tutorial. However, if what became an eventual moat, was indeed an earlier feature, this could have been an enclosure ditch as part of a ditch system around the whole of Hill Close with the Milton brook on the north side, a ditch and marshland to the east, and a ditch running parallel with Fen Road on the south side – this latter feature is indicated today with a ditch and embankment around Hill Close becoming more apparent as you walk down Fen Road in the direction of the River Cam. Such an earlier enclosure ditch's function, was likely to have been a defensive boundary to a prehistoric, Roman or Anglo-Saxon settlement."

Saxon buildings and cemeteries in Milton?

At this point in his tutorial, Tom at last had a perspective on the Anglo-Saxon origins of his village Milton, starting around 1500 years ago. But, there was a great need to find more substantial archaeological evidence for the Anglo-Saxons in Milton through excavations at some time in the future – where were the buildings and cemeteries? In the last few minutes of his tutorial, Dr Crowfoot was going to summarize the Anglo-Saxons in Milton to the wider context of these people in East Anglia and to Britain as a whole, and what we might expect to find in Milton at a future date with regard to the presence of the Anglo-Saxons.

Saxon activity further away

"Although the archaeological evidence for the presence of the Anglo-Saxons in Milton is limited Tom", commented Dr Crowfoot, "when more evidence is discovered, it is likely to conform to that found in other villages within a few miles of Milton. For example, cemeteries both early Saxon pagan with grave goods as found at Oakington, over many years of excavations, and Christian Saxon as found at Trumpington where in 2012 the grave of a young woman of apparent high status was discovered in a field close to the parish church by the Cambridge University Archaeological Unit. Under the chin of the skull and resting on the chest, was a beautiful gold cross intricately inlaid with garnets. The cross was only the fifth of its kind found in Britain which dated the grave to between 650 and 680 AD – a very early Christian burial.

The pagan Anglo-Saxon period is broadly confined to the mid - 5th century to the mid - 7th century when the pottery was crude, being thrown by hand with bold patterning similar to late Iron Age pottery, rather than on a wheel as in the Roman period, but later in the mid to late Anglo-Saxon period, more refined pottery was formed by the wheel as found at Hill Close; early Anglo-Saxon pottery has yet to be found in Milton, although it has been found in neighbouring areas."

"Gradually, the Anglo-Saxons dispersed throughout England into regions; the possible number of Anglo-Saxon invaders contributed to 10% of the population in southern England, and gradually blended with the native Romano-British inhabitants." Dr Crowfoot continued, "in our region of East Anglia, we had the East Angles, now the counties of Essex, Suffolk and Norfolk, and the Middle Angles including Cambridgeshire. To the north east of Milton on the other side of the River Cam, there are two deep ditches (dykes) with embankments running east from the river basin to the higher chalk land. One of these nearest to Milton, at Fen Ditton, is the beginning of the eastern track of the remnants of the Fleam Dyke which runs towards the chalk hills beyond Fulbourn. The other dyke, the Devils Dyke which is much more grand and a dominant feature on the landscape in the direction of Newmarket, runs from the village of Reach to wooded hills south east of Newmarket near Ditton Green – a distance of around 7 miles. These two dykes were dug by the Anglo-Saxons as defensive ditches and embankments separating the Middle Angles from the East Angles.

To the west of the Middle Angles, was the great Anglo-Saxon kingdom of Mercia which spread across the Midlands to the Welsh border, a notable king was Offa who was converted to Christianity and built Offa's dyke as a defensive feature against the Celtic Welsh. At the centre of Mercia were the middle England settlements of Lichfield and Tamworth with good communication routes of rivers and the Roman road called Watling Street – now the A5. In 2009, Terry Herbert using a metal detector in a field close to Lichfield and near the A5 and M6 roads, discovered a large hoard of Anglo-Saxon gold artefacts representing military items (helmet, sword fittings etc.), but also Christian crosses, one with a biblical quotation. The hoard is known as the Staffordshire hoard. It seems therefore that we have on the one hand in the hoard, artefacts as splendid as the finds associated with the pagan Anglo-Saxon ship burial at Sutton Hoo, in Suffolk, and on the other hand, those of the Christian Anglo-Saxon period. The full significance of the mixed period finds in the Staffordshire hoard has yet to be resolved pending detailed professional analysis. Were they the consequence of a battle between pagan and early Christian Anglo-Saxon tribes during the dramatic transition period in Anglo-Saxon culture in Britain during the late 7th century?"

Danes nearby in Cambridge

Dr Crowfoot then returned to the context of Cambridge in the Dark Ages, dealing with the late Anglo-Saxon period leading up to the Norman Conquest. " Tom," Dr Crowfoot continued, "By the 8th century, the influence of King Offa had spread to East Anglia with the building of a fortified bridge over the River Cam at Cambridge. This bridge was captured by the Danes in 875 AD who constructed a new bridge over the river when Cambridge came under the Dane Law. The Danish army which paved the way for the Danish command of East Anglia, was under King Guthrum as recorded in the Anglo-Saxon Chronicle of around 880

AD; this kingdom became known as the Eastern Danelaw. The towns Cambridge, Huntingdon, Bedford and Northampton, under the Danelaw, later became the county towns of the respective 'shire' counties. It is likely that the Danes imposed their own system of farming and an agrarian economy based on strip farming within the Anglo-Saxon open fields. This also led to the nucleation of distinct communities through the cooperation of strip farmers who under the Anglo-Saxons, had been dispersed as hamlets – the villages as we know them today were finally established so that by the Norman Conquest, there were around 160 villages in Cambridgeshire. Later in 917 AD, the Anglo-Saxon, Edward the Elder defeated the Danes and developed Cambridge as a town to the south of the river which continued expanding to the present day; so we have three periods in the development of post Roman Cambridge which would have embraced Milton i.e. the Mercian, Danish and English. It was during the late Anglo-Saxon period before the Norman Conquest that the land was divided into Hundreds and parishes with Milton becoming a parish in the Hundred of Northstowe."

Land ownership before the Norman Conquest

Tom was fascinated by the changing face of Milton during the Dark Ages following the Roman occupation, and particularly the competing influences of the Germanic invaders including the Viking Danes towards the end of the Dark Ages before the Norman Conquest, which to Tom indicated a complex situation with land ownership at this time; this led Tom to pose the obvious question, "Dr Crowfoot, who were the landowners at the time of the Norman Conquest in 1066?" In reply to this important question, Dr Crowfoot said to Tom, "I am glad you have asked this question, because the answer is an introduction to our tutorial next Saturday when we will consider the impact the Normans had on Milton. Abbot Thurcytel expelled from Bedford in 971 AD, gave over 4 hides of land at Milton to the canons of St Paul's,

London in return for a prebend there. But the clerks finding their possession uncertain, exchanged the land before 984 AD, for land in Essex with the new founded abbey at Ely. Beorthnoth (Brithnothus) the abbot of Ely who died soon after in about 996 AD, acquired a further 2 hides at Milton from a person Ulf in exchange for land at Fordham in east Cambridgeshire. The abbey's Milton estate, subsequently comprised the whole village of 12 hides. By 1066, over 6 hides had been given to Aethelbeorht (Ailbertus) the abbey's steward and another nearly 5 hides being in the possession of 4 sokemen (soke was a Danish division of land, seen today with the Soke of Peterborough). All the land with a further area of yardlands (around 3) held by a royal sokeman, had by 1086 following the Norman Conquest, been taken by the notorious sheriff Picot. So Tom, the landownership at Milton by the 11th century was quite complicated as you can see. But there we shall leave our tutorial on the Dark Ages dominated by the Anglo-Saxons, and look forward to a more constructive period in our history supported by some artefact information following the Norman Conquest which we will consider next Saturday."

Dr Crowfoot then let the embers in the fire grate run low, until being revived later in the day for he and his wife to appreciate, as they relaxed in the old Victorian chairs either side of the fireplace in the evening; furthermore, Caesar the cat might be allowed in the room to absorb the heat from the fire as he dozed off to sleep on the mat. Tom meanwhile said goodbye to Dr Crowfoot and his wife, as he set off along Fen Road on his bicycle towards home, the cold wind and rain now thankfully abated, so that he could enjoy the rest of the day playing football at the local recreation ground, and relaxing his mind before college again on Monday.

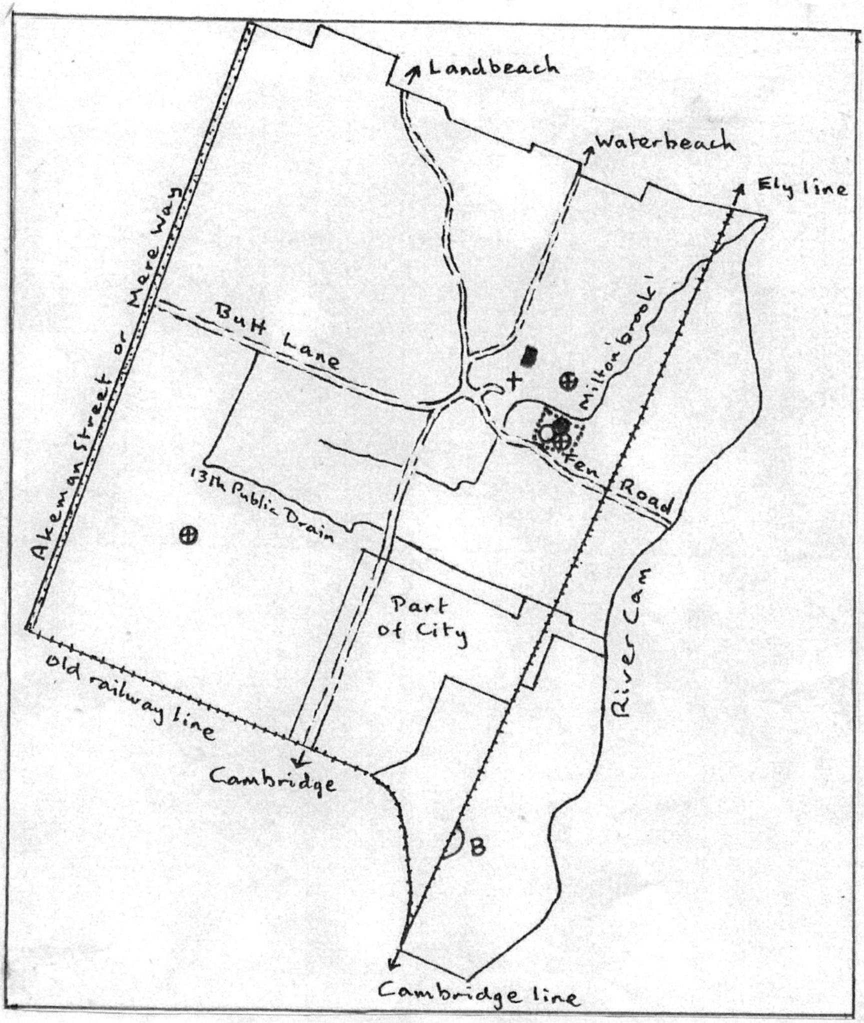

31. Anglo-Saxon distribution of finds.

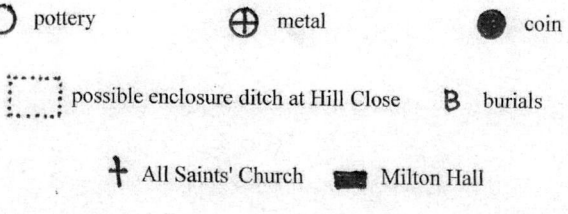

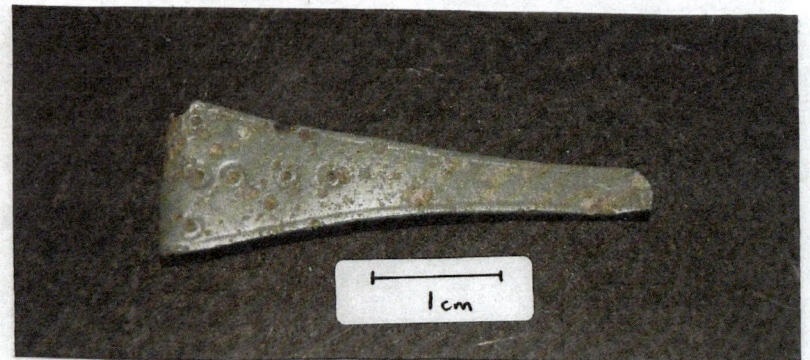

32. Anglo-Saxon part tweezers found at Hill Close, Milton.

33. Anglo-Saxon re-use of an Arles mint Roman coin with hole made for possible use in a necklace of coins found at Hill Close, Milton.

34. Anglo-Saxon high status Ipswich ware pottery (9th century) found at Hill Close, Milton.

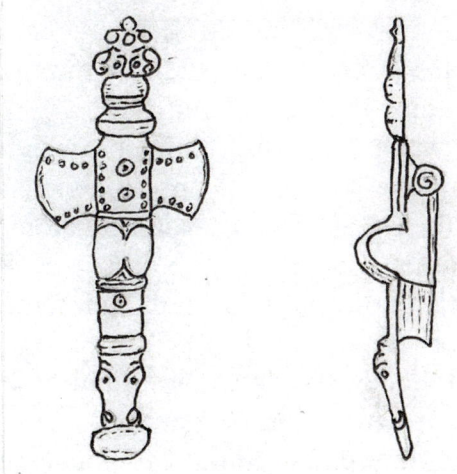

35. typical Anglo-Saxon cruciform brooch <u>yet</u> to be found in Milton.

(note human head at top and boar's head at bottom)

5. Normans - 'still with us'

This Saturday morning could not have been more different to the previous Saturday. Although the days were rapidly getting shorter, instead of the cold wind and rain of a week ago, Tom was awakened by the sunrise as streaks of sunlight broke through the gap in his bedroom curtains. Outside the air was clear and still, and not too cold for late autumn; this atmosphere provided a back-up to the time registering on Tom's bedside clock – 8 o'clock, the sound of the bell from All Saints' Church clock rang out 8 chimes penetrating through the slightly open flap-window of the bedroom with that distinct impact of a determined, yet distant echoing sound. As Tom quickly arose and switched on to the world with that trio – a shower, dressing and breakfast, he had the feeling that today's tutorial was going to complement the inspiring dawn of this morning. Tom was going to be introduced to a new and enlightening millenium in the development through time of Milton, and somehow the sound of the church clock bell this morning, was heralding this new dimension.

Tom prompt as usual, was sitting in his chair by the fire at Kiln Cottage a few minutes after 9.00 am, enjoying his coffee and home made biscuit. Caesar the cat would liked to have occupied the chair on the other side of the fireplace, but as Dr Crowfoot entered the room, he lowered his tail and with a guilty look scurried out of the room.

With both tutor and student comfortably settled in their respective seats, Dr Crowfoot commenced the tutorial starting where the previous Saturday's tutorial had concluded with the end of the Dark Ages and the Anglo-Saxon influence over the inhabitants of Milton. Dr Crowfoot with a pensive look said, "Tom, today we will begin to move away from direct archaeology just finding artefacts on the surface of the soil during fieldwalks or through excavations, we will be considering more substantial artefacts such as buildings and landscape features.

The Normans import a new order

Following the Battle of Hastings in 1066 when William Duke of Normandy defeated the Anglo-Saxon King Harold, this brought about the end of Anglo-Saxon rule in England and a new and more sophisticated culture was imposed on our island. New laws, substantial buildings such as churches, cathedrals, monasteries and castles were built, many still with us today, functional or ruins as legacies of the past 1000 years. In 1086, a nationwide census of the population and its distribution in relation to most aspects of occupation, was carried out which led to the publication of the 'Domesday Book'; at this time Milton acquired its Norman – French name of Middeltone, in the Hundred of Cestretone (Chesterton) – later Northstowe and the County of Grentebrigscine (Cambridgeshire); the population was less than 50. A new language was introduced to us – Norman French, which over time welded with the Germanic tongues of Anglo-Saxon, Norse Viking and some remnants of our indigenous Celtic language and Latin from the Romans; the result of all this blending eventually led to the English language as we know it today.

All Saints' Church established

But first, what did the Normans initially do for Milton which has had an effect still with us today?" Tom, still in his mind-set of pottery sherds and coins in the fields, thought hard for a moment – then an image of stone and mortar came into his head, All Saints' Church, this is an artefact and very old! Cautiously, Tom exclaimed, "Was it our parish church?" Whereupon, Dr Crowfoot replied, "you are absolutely right Tom, it was indeed the building of our local church, which as alluded to earlier, was built on the likely site of an earlier timber Anglo-Saxon church. Therefore, the first part of our tutorial this morning will be devoted to a description of the architectural features of our parish church as they have appeared over time, and some of the people who have been closely associated with the church during this time such as certain lords of the manor; the manor will be the other major topic to be considered today and this will take us back to some field archaeology. So let us begin, I have a ground plan of the present church which I will refer to as I describe the various features of the architecture and some fittings" Dr Crowfoot then began his description of the church.

Dr Crowfoot referred to the main sources of information on the church, the first being the Rev William Keating Clay's book published by the Cambridge Antiquarian Society in 1869, 'A History of the Parish of Milton in the County of Cambridge'. The second important source of information, is 'The Victoria History of the Counties of England: Milton and other estates in A History of the County of Cambridgeshire and the Isle of Ely: Volume 9, 1989' and finally, a third source of information is the 'Buildings of England, Cambridgeshire' by Nikolaus Pevsner, published by Penguin books, 1954. Dr Crowfoot then informed Tom that these publications are readily available in the Cambridge Collection at the Cambridgeshire Library in the city, and that he would now summarize the essential details.

The church consists of a chancel, nave, south aisle, north aisle, a south porch and a west tower and is constructed of Barnack limestone, ashlar and plastered rubble; there is a modern pentagonal church hall extension (completed in 1984) attached to the north side of the church. The whole site is situated 7.64 m AOD on a plateau of land with a fully occupied grave yard since 1897, surrounding the church.

The porch and nave

The main entrance to the church is through the south porch, which is a relatively modern construction built around the middle of the

19th century replacing an earlier porch. As you enter the church, on the right of the main door and on the south wall, is mounted a slightly coped, tapering stone coffin lid (1.65 m in length) probably of the 13th century with a central shaft terminating in fleury crosses at both ends and opposing horseshoe images placed centrally. The coffin lid was originally found in the nave in 1864 when major renovations were carried out in the church, and until recently was on the floor to the left of the main entrance. Inside and above the main door, is a Royal Coat of Arms transferred from All Saints' Church, Landbeach in 1826. Also to the right of the main entrance, stands the octagonal stone font, one of the oldest features in the church in the style of the 12th century; the cover is Jacobean, 17th century and the figure 8 (octagon) in the Middle Ages symbolised regeneration.

Looking up at the barrel roof, the 17th century roof is on moulded tiebeams with pendants and was covered by a ceiling to reduce the loss of heat in the church; until the reign of Elizabeth I in the 16th century, the roof was thatched. The nave is three bayed with arcades formed from round shafts on square piers which support moulded arches, and was possibly rebuilt in the early 14th century.

Turning right, is the main part of the nave which is now an open feature after the removal of the pews at the end of the 20th century, being replaced with moveable single chairs, therefore allowing for flexible arrangements of seating. Prior to this work, the then Hertfordshire Archaeological Trust (now Archaeological Solutions Ltd), were contracted to make an archaeological evaluation of the nave in 1999 before it was lowered by 0.25 m as part of the alterations.

Archaeology in the nave

An L-shaped linear trench was opened with the north-south trench measuring 7.5 m in length and 0.5 m wide, the east-west trench was 7.0 m in length and 0.3 m wide; both trenches were 0.65 m deep. The following notable observations were made within the trenches. Stone blocks had been laid directly beneath the pews and base soil was exposed consisting of a mid-brown silty loam with inclusions of sub-angular flints and stones, glass fragments, nails and disarticulated human bone fragments representing disturbed medieval layers. There were also some square encaustic (glazed clay) floor tiles (red, yellow and grey), associated with cement and decayed lime mortar for realigning tiles in the 19th century. No articulated human bone was found associated with a distinct grave site, but if there were any graves, these could have been at a depth below the excavation. Later work in 2001, revealed more earlier building debris, fragments of human remains, coffin nails and one coffin handle, and fragments of Victorian bottle glass; bases of the arcade piers and surrounding wall footings (14th century) were also revealed, some strengthened at different times, but there was no evidence of earlier features. The nave pillars are of the early decorated period while the tracery of the windows above the south aisle are of the late decorated period (13th century); the windows each have three lights.

The chancel

The nave is separated from the chancel by a Romanesque arch, of the Norman period, date - late 11th or early 12th century, and therefore likely to be the earliest existing structure in the church. Passing through the arch into the chancel, this was built in the late 13th century probably replacing an earlier Norman apse, but apart from the south wall, the remainder including the east window was restored in 1847 with donations from the patrons King's College. The four rows of choir stalls have carved hinged seats (misericords) which can be dated by the carving of a bishop's head with a 15th century mitre carved on the arm of the right hand seat; these seats were initially made for the clergy who had to stand for long periods, but they could rest on the edge of the hinged seats without lowering them to the full seating position. Note, on the oldest south wall of the chancel, the 13th century piscina or bowl where sacred vessels were rinsed, and also the sedilia – recessed stone seats for the clergy dated to about 1500 in the reign of Henry VII, because of the presence of the double feathering ornamentation. In front of the altar, the communion rail which dates from the 17th century, arose as surplus from King's College as patrons of the parish since the reign of Elizabeth I. Despite opposition through the persuasive influence of our local curate and antiquary William Cole, over the Provost of King's, the rails were installed in 1779. To the north of the altar is the memorial brass to Sir William Coke and his family. Coke (or Cooke/Cook) was a significant judge in England during the 16th century being a Lord Chief Justice of the King's bench, and also one time lord of the manor of Milton. Also on a stone, on the floor near the altar, is a faint inscription to the memory of the wife of a former rector of Milton, John Lane, who died in 1743. On the north and south walls are tablets to the Rev O Naylor and his wife, both of the 18th century. Like the misericords, the vestry door is finely carved and originated together with its stone surround from the old rectory on the site of the later rectory built in 1846, (which is now part of the childrens' hospice 'Each' since the early 1980's; this necessitated the building of yet another rectory in the garden of the old rectory). The east window is modern with four lights in the decorated style, but the north and south windows are late perpendicular; the 19th century glass in the south window depicts the sacrament of the Lord's Supper and the marriage supper of Cana of Galilee. Finally, the open roof is a copy of that in the Roman Catholic chapel in Cambridge by Pugin, the notable 19th century architect.

The north aisle

Leaving the chancel, on the right is the north aisle. It was here in the 18th century that William Cole had his own pew which occupied the whole of the east end of the north aisle; earlier this would have been the customary side chapel found in parish churches. But, by 1779 this aisle had deteriorated so much that it was pulled down much to the disgust of Cole, and not rebuilt, in the same style, until 1847. Before the modern church hall was annexed to the church in the 1980's, there was a large east window in the north aisle (where the door now leads into the church hall). This window contained some significant stained glass donated by William Cole, unfortunately, its whereabouts is not known, But, it is worth recalling the composition of the window as it was recorded by the Rev W Clay in 1869, and likewise by Dr William Palmer (physician and antiquary) in his book on 'William Cole of Milton', published by Galloway & Porter in 1935 (facsimile reprint 2007, Cambridge University Press, edited by Dr John Pickles). Quote, "In this window may be seen at the present time (1935), six pieces of painted glass, the sole known remains of Cole's large collection. Just below the tracery, one on each side, are the Royal Arms of the sixteenth century. Between them is a Tudor rose. Beneath the latter is a representation of the death of Ananias and Sapphira (the exposure of their sin by Peter *Acts 5:10*), and in the side lights are two round pieces with figures of the Saints Margaret and Catherine". On the north wall is a tablet, 'In memory of Isaac Marsh died 1837, age 65'.

The south aisle

Walking across the nave from the north aisle brings us to the south aisle, where there are several monuments. Incidentally, following the archaeological survey carried out on the nave as mentioned earlier, the floor of the church was lowered by 0.25 m beyond the nave to include the north and south aisles. The south aisle is the oldest part of the church remaining after the chancel arch, and dates from the early decorated style at around 1220. During repair work in 1845, some small images were discovered in the south wall which had been concealed during the Reformation, but their whereabouts today, is not known; the position of this find is represented by a niche in the wall. The pear moulding over an arch in the south wall is also likely to be around 1220. The east window in the south aisle includes three coats of arms: one with six quarterings suggests an association with Queens' College because these are the arms of Queen Margaret of Anjou, wife of Henry VI, and one of the founders of Queens'. The window with twenty two quarterings, is that belonging to an earlier Baron Maltravers. There are some old pieces of painted glass in other windows on the south aisle.

Archaeology of the south aisle – the vault

During the return visit by the Hertfordshire Archaeological Trust in 2001, attention was given to the vault beneath the raised floor in the south east corner of the south aisle. This vault is entered by six steps of 0.92 m width and 0.3 m depth located to the right of the south porch which descend to a total depth of around 1.5 m (the entrance is now concealed under the raised floor of the south aisle). The vault roof is plain and semi-circular, constructed of brick and limewash. A stone slab is raised from the floor by brick partitions, these partitions provide for three cavities, each containing a lead coffin covered in wood, which on examination was now mostly decayed as they lay in about 2cm of ground water. The three coffins on the upper stone shelf had more wood remaining, as well as some upholstery studs and fabric with name plates, but these too were considerably decayed. No further investigation was attempted. A stray find, was a human leg bone in bad condition on the flooded floor, probably related to an earlier burial on the site. The vault was constructed for the Knight family (members were both rectors and lords of the manor, to be dealt with later). During construction, there could have been destruction of earlier burials on the site as indicated above, however the vault is an interesting example of a semi-aristocratic family tomb.

The incumbants of the vault are the Rev Samuel Knight (rector and lord of the manor, died 1790); his grandson's wife, Elizabeth Knight, died 1800; his grandson Samuel, died 1829; his son Samuel (lord of the manor, died 1835). Elizabeth Knight's sister Sarah Spelman is the fifth occupant of the vault, died 1806, while the sixth coffin may be that of a third sister of Elizabeth, Anne Spelman, died 1835.

Memorial monuments

Memorial monuments to members of the Knight family are present on the south wall as follows: Rev Samuel Knight who died in 1790, a marble relief to Elizabeth who died in 1800 was produced by Flaxman, one of England's most famous sculptors. The memorial depicts Elizabeth's spirit being raised to heaven by an angel, but in this early work, the angel has no wings, and finally, Samuel Knight who died in 1835. Another fine sculpture is on the west wall, to the Rev Samuel Knight, died 1829, produced by Sir R Chantrey and represents the descent of the Holy Spirit. Part of the south aisle was partitioned off from the nave in the 18th century as the manor chapel, and records report a chapel here as early as 1279; this chapel was once called L'Estrange's Chapel who was lord of the manor in 1279. There is a piscina on the south wall above which there was a memorial stone with a brass plate to the Harris family who were lords of the manor in the 17th century. There is however, another brass tablet on the east wall to the Harris family with a coat of arms, indicating several members of this family are buried nearby; perhaps the leg bone and inferred burials disturbed during the construction of the Knight's vault mentioned above, are indicators of the Harris burials? In the north corner of the south aisle is an 19th century monument to George Nichols and family, and to Anne Spelman who died in 1935. Above the pulpit is a memorial plague to those men of Milton who lost their lives in the Great War of 1914-1918.

Ledger stones of York stone approximately 5 cm thick situated under the pews to the north of the south aisle, were investigated by the Hertfordshire Archaeological Trust. The ledger stones had partly erased inscriptions indicating burials beneath the stones. The most legible inscription was on the western stone in 1869 as follows, 'Here lieth the body of William Kettle who dyed the 30th day of June 1700 in the 69th year of his age. Catherine his wife died 20 August 1727 aged 86 years'. The eastern stone with less inscription, had the truncated remains of leg bones immediately below the stone, suggesting the presence of a skeleton beneath the slab, but at a different alignment. No traces of a coffin were found, but the significance of the bones was not further investigated. The ledger stones are now concealed under the raised floor of the south aisle. Finally, the early decorated roof of the south aisle was repaired at the expense of John Percy Baumgartner, lord of the manor, in 1855.

The tower

The remaining part of the structure of the church to be examined is best seen from outside, this is the tower. Essentially the tower dates from the late decorated period with two stage buttresses on the southwest and northwest corners of the tower, and three stage buttresses both later, and the highest, on the north and south corners of the tower. On the south face of the tower is a human head carved in stone (this may have originally been over the east window of the chancel). The upper part of the tower has a plain battlement parapet which has been raised on two occasions. The steeple once had a pigeon house accessed by square holes cut into the tower. There is a clock present only on the west face of the tower. This was installed in 1848 at a cost of £53 as compensation from the Great Eastern Railway for parish land taken for the construction of the London to King's Lynn rail track in Milton Fen. The clock now has an electric mechanism so that it does not have to be wound by hand.

Within the tower are four bells: one, a treble made by Miles Graye in 1665; a second, made by Thomas Newman of Norwich in 1717; a third, possibly made by Tobias Norris of Stamford with the Latin inscription, *'Non clamor sed amor cantat in aure Dei'* (Not noise but love sounds in the ear of God). A fourth bell was added when the bells were rehung in 1926. Viewed from the nave, at the junction with the tower, is the organ, dedicated in 1911 which replaced a barrel organ in use since the 1840's; around 1959, expensive repairs were carried out on the instrument.

A final comment to be made about the church, is that until 1845, the church had both a rector and a vicar living in separate residences. The last vicarage was to the west of the church and became a dilapidated cottage in 1802, leaving only a replacement rectory to be built on the same site in 1846 as mentioned earlier. One other feature of religious interest in the village, was a medieval cross at the centre of the village; unfortunately no traces of its whereabouts are known.

"Well Tom, our tutorial concerned with our parish church has finished," Dr Crowfoot exclaimed with a relieved smile. "One morning or afternoon at a weekend, or during the next school holidays, we will visit the church so that you can see many of those features I have introduced to you today. We will also note some of the more distinctive graves in the churchyard related to notable people living in Milton since the 19th century.

The manor

But now, we must continue with our tutorial to consider another institution in the village which has been with us, at least as long as the church, what do you think this might be Tom?" This question completely vexed Tom, he knew there was no ruined castle or monastery in Milton, so what could it be? Dr Crowfoot seeing a rather blank look on Tom's face, and not wanting to waste any further time, because there was so much information to cram into this day's tutorial spanning a number of centuries, brought relief to

Tom's dilemma. Dr Crowfoot said, "Tom, I am sure you have heard of Milton Hall, that large building surrounded by trees behind the church and now occupied for high-technical industry, well that is the final manor house building in Milton, built at the end of the 18th century. It is the manor which is the next important institution after the church that we are now going to consider."

"You will recall Tom," Dr Crowfoot continued, "in the last tutorial on the Anglo-Saxons as founders of Milton, we reviewed the complicated landownership before the Norman Conquest of 1066. The main landowners before the Conquest were the church and the monasteries, and the monarch and the aristocracy – the most senior people in the country such as those of leading military ranks and lawyers. It was from the latter group of people, that lords of the manor arose, bestowed with significant ownership of land and a large house in which to reside at the centre of a village. Sometimes, there would be more than one lord of the manor with his or her manor in a village i.e. at Fulbourn, but in Milton there was only one.

The Victoria County History for Cambridgeshire which includes Milton, provides a detailed account of all the lords of the manor down through the centuries starting with the Anglo-Saxon Aethelbeorht acting as the abbot of Ely's steward in 1066, followed by the notorious Norman sheriff, Picot in 1086, and ending with John Percy Baumgartner in the 19th century to 1859. Baumgartner's two daughters retained manorial rights into the early 20th century with landownership, but they no longer lived in the manor house, the existing Milton Hall. Now Tom, as it is the purpose of these tutorials to concentrate on artefacts including buildings and landscapes, we will only refer to certain lords of the manor as they are important key people in the material context of the development of Milton; we have already made some mention of this with reference to All Saints' Church and the Knight family." Tom by now was trying to envisage how this part of the morning's tutorial was going to develop in the wake of the Norman Conquest, and so he sat back in his chair with paper and pencil, ready to follow the account that Dr Crowfoot had diligently prepared.

The first manor house

"To start our passage through time on the development of the manor and the location of the associated manor houses," Dr Crowfoot commented, "we must go back to our last tutorial for the first potential archaeological evidence for a manor site during the late Anglo-Saxon period. You will recall Tom, that at the western end of Hill Close, a few sherds of mid to late Saxon pottery were found during the fieldwalk in 2007, and that these finds included 'high status' Ipswich ware. Now the location of these finds was in the area of the supposed 'Hall' or manor house as indicated on the earlier Ordnance Survey maps. A hall building of timber and thatch, would be the Anglo-Saxon equivalent to a manor house, and not far from a timber built church on the site of the present All Saints' Church. However, Tom, the few pottery sherds may only be associated with a more general Anglo-Saxon settlement, rather than a distinct, senior ranking Anglo-Saxon chieftain's residence, only future excavations might put this in perspective.

But, we do have more substantial information and archaeological evidence for a distinct post-Norman Conquest manor at the western end of Hill Close." At this point in the tutorial, Dr Crowfoot embarked on a detailed account of the development of the manor at Milton.

Archival information states that in 1235, Henry III provided the lord of the manor, Godfrey of Crowcombe with ten timbers to build himself a house on manorial land at Milton. It has been assumed that the house was built at Hill Close because of the presence of the large moat feature here which at one time was rectangular. Furthermore, in 1780 the antiquarian William Cole who was living in a large farmhouse a few hundred yards from this site (Milton House) in Fen Road, also found fish ponds, ditches and building foundations, all indicative of a medieval manorial site. But, until recently, no archaeological evidence was available to support a manor site at Hill Close other than that of a possible late Saxon settlement as mentioned above.

Archaeological evidence

At the same time as the Saxon pottery sherds were found at the western end of Hill Close during the fieldwalk in 2007, several sherds of the Saxo-Norman period through to 1400 were found; most of these sherds were medieval sandy grey ware from jugs and jars. However, of particular note was the finding of a relatively large number of Sible Hedingham (green glazed on an oxidised fabric) sherds, a north Essex style of medieval pottery, date 1200-1350. The finding of the predominant Hedingham ware concentrated in the area of the supposed manor house of 1235, is the first definitive archaeological evidence supporting the presence of this early manor house. Furthermore, a large number of oyster shells were found in the same area of Hill Close, providing additional evidence for a high status settlement here.

Additional archaeological evidence for a medieval settlement on the site of the supposed 13th century manor house, was obtained from a 2m x 1m test pit excavation carried out in 2008 by Derek Booth our parish archaeological warden, with the assistance of Active 8 Archaeology. The test pit was dug at the truncation of a large deep ditch feature which could have been part of the eastern side of the moat, and another ditch. Significant finds were 21 medieval pottery sherds weighing 284g, and one other sherd which was Roman; several bones and teeth from large domestic animals such as pig, cattle and sheep were also found. One notable pig find was part of the upper jaw with a small tusk and premolar teeth. This find suggested it came from an early type of adult female pig, typical of a domestic animal with wild boar features, in keeping with a medieval context. Other random artefacts associated with a medieval site, were (a) the finding of a small horseshoe on the soil surface, typical of the post Norman period, (b) a medieval micaceous whetstone, and (c) a large sandstone cornerstone, suggestive of a foundation stone for a timber framed house. There were two other medieval finds, one a copper alloy spoon, the other a long-cross silver penny, date 1279-1489. These finds and several Tudor buttons were also found, but many away from the supposed site of the medieval manor house.

Dr Crowfoot then rounded off his dealing with the first manor house site in Milton by saying, "Tom, it is an interesting question how long the 13th century manor house was occupied, and whether it was restored and improved during the next few centuries? Perhaps a timber frame was replaced by masonry, if so, there seems to be no substantial base walls remaining according to geophysical surveys, alternatively all masonry might have been removed for building the next manor house in the 16th century." Tom was impressed by the way the archaeological data, only found so recently, had been the first archaeological evidence for the supposed site of the medieval manor house in Milton, but now where was the site for the next manor house? Before Dr Crowfoot uttered his first words on the location of the next manor house, Tom interrupted by saying, "Dr Crowfoot, I recall from seeing pictures of parish churches, that there is often a large house very close to the church, and they were referred to as the manor house with sometimes other outbuildings constituting the manor farm nearby, was this the location of Milton's second manor house?" Dr Crowfoot replied by saying to Tom, "you are an observant lad, the later manor houses were very close to the parish church so that the lord of the manor and his family did not have far to walk to church, also the lord of the manor was sometimes the rector, particulary from the 16th century. This situation arose in Milton, so let us take a look at the second manor house."

The second manor house

"The building of the second manor house at Milton," Dr Crowfoot continued, "was initiated by the judge and lord of the manor William Cook in about 1550, some 300 years since the first manor house was built at Hill Close in the 13th century. It was also a time when the political climate in England was going through a very unstable period involving the Reformation with the establishment of the Protestant Church of England, including All Saints' Church, under Henry VIII. In the process, the land that was sold enabled grand houses to be built; it is possible that a new manor house for Milton was one of these. The exact location of the new manor house remains elusive, but it seems it was very close, to the north side of the church, and an indication of its size is realized from the description of the number of rooms within the building as recorded in the Victoria County History for Cambridgshire. It is from this point in our story, that archaeological evidence is lacking, being replaced by the historical evidence associated with architectural features of the manor house.

Cook's manor house consisted of at least three main rooms, the largest being the 'hall room' with a gallery; by the 1660's, there were up to 10 fire places, and there were offices and cellars to the south of the main house. A century later in 1772 when the manor house was being repaired, William Cook's initials were found carved on an arched doorway, and fragments of old stonework were discovered. I wonder where this old stonework originated, any ideas Tom?" Tom had heard of masonry being taken from old buildings to be used in new buildings, particularly when the monasteries were destroyed during their Dissolution under Henry VIII, and the stones then being incorporated into the new houses of the new landowners. Tom with this knowledge from his school history lessons, replied to Dr Crowfoot's question, "perhaps some of the stones in the new manor house came from local monastic buildings destroyed at the Dissolution, such as Denny Abbey and from foundations of the 13th century manor house at Hill Close?" "You could be right here Tom," exclaimed Dr Crowfoot, "particularly if the first manor house had been restored from being primarily a timber framed building, to one with more masonry a century or two later. It is worth noting that during the excavations by OAE on the land behind the second and later final manor house, medieval pottery (11th to 14th century), was found mainly to the northwest, and may not be related to the those living at the manor house, but to other village dwellings. Subsequent excavations by Essex County Council archaeologists in 2013, found more medieval pottery at the northwestern corner of the site, suggesting that indeed, there could possibly have been a medieval hamlet here by the old Ely Road. Furthermore, the Essex group exposed courses of Tudor bricks and some stone immediately north of the present Milton Hall; these courses suggested foundations of outbuildings, perhaps stables for the Hall, reusing bricks and stone from the demolished Tudor manor house. In this context, skeletal remains of modern horses were found in excavations nearby. Alternatively, these foundations could perhaps be part of the Tudor manor house."

Dr Crowfoot went on to say that the second manor house existed as such with a succession of lords of the manor, many related to each other, until about 1767 when a new lord of the manor, the Rev Samuel Knight bought the manor house for £10,000 including over 487 acres of land from the previous lord of the manor, the Rev Jeremy Pemberton; the Pemberton family had used the manor house as a farm house, but the Rev Samuel Knight preferred to live in the house as a manor house, rather than the rectory to the south of the church.

The third manor house

However, the days of the second manor house were now limited. Within a few years of the Rev Samuel Knight becoming lord of the manor, his son also Samuel Knight, began to build in 1772, yet another manor house in Milton, the third and last in the village. During the building of this house, the Knight family continued to live in the old manor house adjacent to the new building which was completed in 1794 by which time, the Rev Samuel Knight had died and was buried in the vault in All Saints' Church as mentioned earlier. The Georgian manor house was built of local yellow-grey bricks in a neo-classical external style. The visual impact of the house portrays a large, essentially square building with a three-storeyed centre part containing a balconied room on the top floor. The ground floor consists of a 40 ft high hall on the west side, and to the east there is an oval room projecting as a bow towards the park. These rooms are flanked by two large rooms used in 1800 as the drawing and dining rooms respectively, and by two-storeyed wings containing offices. West and North lodges were built in the late 19th century. At the end of the 18th century as shown on the Enclosure Award map of 1802, there were three ponds to the southeast of the church and rectory, and adjacent to the north side of the Milton brook. It is highly likely that these were the manorial fish ponds supplying carp and other fish for the manor house, particularly for Cook's manor house. Today there is just one small pond remaining as part of the terraced flower and shrub garden in 'Each' children's hospice grounds.

With the detailed description of this last manor house in Milton being described to Tom by Dr Crowfoot, Dr Crowfoot then posed another thought for Tom to consider. "When we talk of a manor, is this just the building of the house?" Dr Crowfoot said to Tom. After a short pause, Tom replied, " doesn't this also imply land as well?" Whereupon, the expression on Dr Crowfoot's face indicated that a positive response was forthcoming. "You are right here again Tom, a manor consists of the house and variable amounts of land. We shall see that by the end of this morning's session, the land associated with the manor at Milton in relation to other land ownership in the village, has changed by the end of the 18th century. It will be the land in the context of landscape which will feature widely in the remainder of the whole tutorial course.

Land closest to the Hall

But first, let us consider the land immediately surrounding this new manor house. In the late 18th century, a new fashion had arisen in the landscaping of the land around distinctive large houses, this fashion was a return to designing a 'natural' landscape with extensive views from the house, in contrast to the formal gardens with flower borders and water fountains distinctive of the previous 16th and 17th centuries. The most well known landscape architect of the 18th century was Lancelot 'Capability' Brown (seeing capabilities in landscape design); one of the most important men of his school, was the East Anglian Humphrey Repton, and it was he who in 1789 was contracted to design the landscape for Milton Hall. Essentially, the house was surrounded by parkland, designed to have large areas of grass with trees scattered across the terrain. So that the Hall had more parkland to the west, the Cambridge to Ely turnpike road built in 1763, which ran in front of the house from Church Lane, was diverted in 1795 to the west as the High Street and Landbeach Road, the latter then turned to the right to continue as the turnpike road to Waterbeach. At this time, a milestone was placed on the left of the turnpike road adjacent to the present allotments, showing the distances to Cambridge, Ely and London.

A large area of open grassland to the east and back of Milton Hall, provided a vista which was terminated by a long copse of trees, mostly horse chestnut running along the edge of Milton Fen on the first terrace alluvium; this landscape exists to the present day. It is interesting to note that there is a deep ditch between the present day lawn behind the eastern side of the Hall and the grassland beyond; this ditch feature suggests it is a 'ha-ha' the name given to a ditch surrounding a large property to deter wandering livestock or even deer from entering the land near the house.

The lake

Now Tom you will recall from our earlier tutorials, that running between the parkland near to the east of the Hall and north of Hill Close, was a small stream which we call the Milton brook, and would have been an important source of water for the earlier civilizations living at Hill Close and Long Meadow. Humphrey Repton took advantage of this water course by having the land immediately around it excavated to form a boating lake. It is possible that the Milton brook may have earlier been the source of water for the construction of fish ponds for the first manor house at Hill Close, the presence of which, William Cole refers to. If this was the case, then we have a situation which we know did occur at Wimpole south of Cambridge where fish ponds were extended to form a lake by 'Capability' Brown. The shape of the lake at Milton, was 'serpentine' from west to east, providing an illusion of a length of a large winding section of a river – a feature to enhance a natural landscape! Furthermore, the grandeur of the feature was likened to the 'Clytumnus River' (named after a tributary of the Tiber in Umbria, Italy. The original river in Italy mentioned by Pliny, was sacred and personified as a god with an ancient Christian temple nearby – in Milton this was All Saints' Church). As mentioned earlier, a small conduit was constructed as an overflow for the lake taking the water into a ditch and away to the Fen and the River Cam. It is of further interest that at the western end of the lake near a small island, there was a spur off the brook towards the manor house and stable block of the rectory, and another running southeast towards the moat at Hill Close. The former diversion may have allowed access for a small boat from the residences to the lake, and the latter for taking water to the moat. Repton's landscaping was completed by 1794."

At this point in the tutorial, Dr Crowfoot had finished the development of the manor houses in Milton up to the end of the 18th century, and turned his attention to the change in land use and hence landscape involving manorial lands from the period just after the Norman Conquest to the Enclosure Act of 1802 for Milton.

"Tom, I would now like to consider a brief summary of the division of the land in Milton as it developed through the period we have been discussing from the building of the post - Norman parish church to the last manor house at Milton." With these words as an introduction, Dr Crowfoot then began to discuss the change in land use over this period of some 700 years as the last topic in this week's tutorial.

Land use

The Domesday survey for Cambridgeshire exists as two versions, one the ecclesiastical (Inquisitio Eliensis – abbots lands), and the other secular (Inquisitio Comitatus Cantabrigiensis – holders of estates). In the Domesday book, an estate is a unit or recording for a particular landowner in a particular place, and most of these were manors (manerium). A village such as Milton is a unit of location or settlement with land usage defined as 'plough lands'.
According to Dr Oliver Rackham, the notable Cambridge botanist and landscape historian, 35% of land in Britain was arable i.e. 81,000 ploughs – 120 acres to a plough worked by oxen, with non ploughing land for cattle, sheep and pigs dispersed between 15% woodland and wood pasture, and 1% meadow; overall pasture was 30% with the remaining 20% of the land consisting of mountains, moors, heaths, fens and buildings etc. Considering the land in Milton had been inhabited and farmed from pre-Roman times, it is likely that much more land than the national average was used for crops and for grazing livestock at the time of the Domesday survey; an indication of this was the extensive field systems which were probably in place by 1300. These field systems described as open fields occupied the western part of the parish with an acreage of around 1120, the remaining fifth of the parish was the fen pastures. There were three principle fields: the largest South Field

(310 acres) between Chesterton parish and Butt Lane, Middle Field (240 acres) north of Butt Lane and Mill Field (410 acres) towards Landbeach. It is of interest that adjacent to Butt Lane in the area once South Field, archaeologists from Oxford Archaeology East, recently discovered the site of a medieval windmill and pottery prior to the site becoming the Milton Park and Ride terminus. East of the present Waterbeach Road from Milton, there was Island field (120 acres). Most of the arable land was divided into 'selions' of half to three quarters of an acre under separate ownership. With reference again to South Field during the archaeology being carried out before the Park and Ride work, ridges towards the southern end of the field were seen as a remnant of medieval ridge and furrow strip farming.

The manorial land existed as larger blocks. For example, by 1600, of 507 acres, 175 was in lots, many 5-7 acres, a 29 acre furlong in Middle Field, and several plots of 10-20 acres each. By the middle of the 17th century, some of the land had become 'pieces' such as Pound Piece (22 acres) to the east of the village off Fen Road. Further east from here was Milton Fen mentioned in 1286 as a permanent pasture (liable to flooding in the winter months). By 1600 the fen had been divided into Land Fen (70 acres), east of Island Field, Lug Fen (35 acres) and Basbitt (named in 1424, later Backsbite then Baitsbite) Fen (55 acres). East of South Field, was Baitsbite Field (55 acres) which occupied the area between the present Cambridge Road and the edge of the 2nd terrace alluvium (Eastern boundary of the present Country Park), with Fen Road to the north and the 13th public drain to the south. Much of the manorial land away from the parkland of the manor, was occupied by tenants who were known a copyholders.

"Our long and varied tutorial on the development of Milton from an archaeological, architectural and land perspective during 700 years from the Norman Conquest to the end of the 18th century, is drawing to a close," Dr Crowfoot, looking rather tired, exclaimed to Tom. "We have just one more aspect to briefly consider in this tutorial, and that is some details about the population and land occupation.

Population and land occupation

By the 13th and 14th centuries, the whole village belonged to the manor except for 50 acres freehold attached to estates in Landbeach, Waterbeach and the glebe. In 1279, there were 5 significant freeholders with a total of 73 acres, 10 others had smaller plots of land. At this time, there were 75 tenants. By 1327, there were 30 resident tax payers, but by 1377, 146 adults paid the poll tax, being reduced to 18 by 1524; this reduction was due to the effect of the plague (Black Death) on the population, and by 1563 there were still only 36 households. In the late 17th century, there were 40 dwellings accommodating 86 adults in 1676. From this time into the 18th century, the population of Milton grew slowly. In 1728 there were 40 families with 170 inhabitants and by 1782 there were still only now 39 dwellings housing 244 people, this increased to 40 dwellings again, but housing now 55 families providing a total population of 270 people in 1800. This increase in population, but not associated with an increase in housing, was due in part to the destruction of the humble timber and thatched cottages being destroyed by the large fire which swept through the village in 1735. In those days the houses in the village were primarily confined to the High Street and Fen Lane (Road) and would have been built quite close together, therefore a reason why the fire spread so quickly.

By 1520, the tenements of the manor had all become copy holders paying 12s rent for half a yardland and 18s for a full 16 acre yardland. Around 1600, about 350 acres were copyhold and 177 acres freehold. However, at enclosure in 1802, only 136 acres of allotments were made from 192 acres of copyhold, the remainder was subsequently enfranchised. During the later middle ages and beyond, some of the land in Milton came into the ownership of several colleges of Cambridge University, such as Pembroke, King's, Gonville and Caius, and Trinity. Also during the middle ages, the name of Milton had changed from Middletone to Middleton by the reign of Edward III, then by the end of Edward's reign, finally to Milton as we know it today."

"In our next tutorial Tom, we will see what effect the Enclosure Act of 1802 for Milton had on the land division as the manor began to relinquish more land for freehold occupation, and the institution of manorial authority in Milton came to an end." With these words, Dr Crowfoot walked to the front door with Tom, followed by Caesar the cat. Tom grabbed his bicycle from the side of the cottage and cycled off along Fen Road, waving to Dr Crowfoot, who had by now reached the front gate and returned a complementary wave. Both tutor and student were relieved that this Saturday morning's marathon session had at last come to an end. Although it had gone beyond the one hour, Tom was pleased that he had been exposed to so much information about the two key institutions in his village, the parish church and the manor, and their significance to the people of Milton over so many centuries.

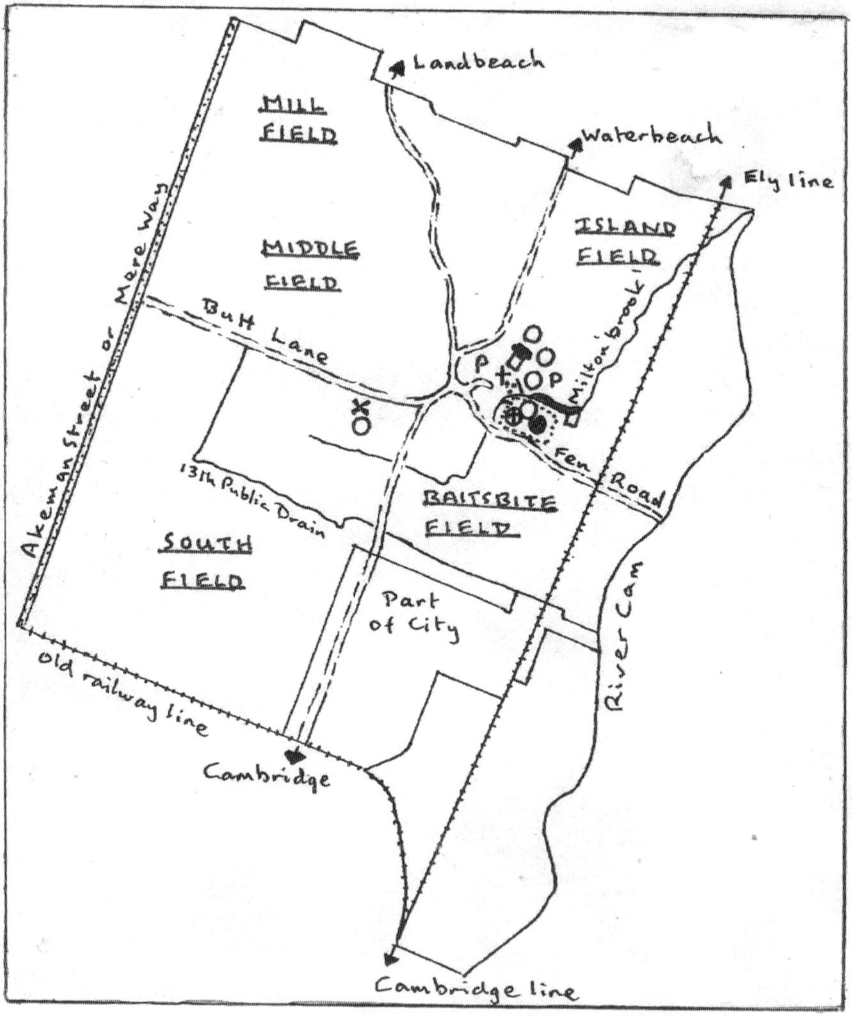

36. Post Norman finds and Manor sites to 1800.

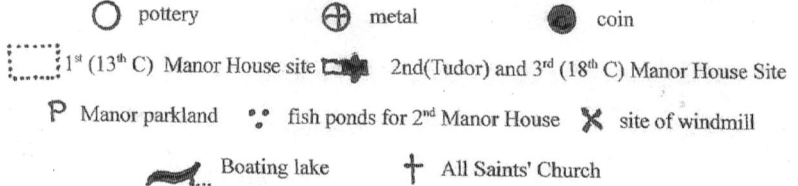

○ pottery ⊕ metal ● coin

▫ 1st (13th C) Manor House site   ▰ 2nd (Tudor) and 3rd (18th C) Manor House Site

P Manor parkland   •• fish ponds for 2nd Manor House   ✕ site of windmill

～ Boating lake   † All Saints' Church

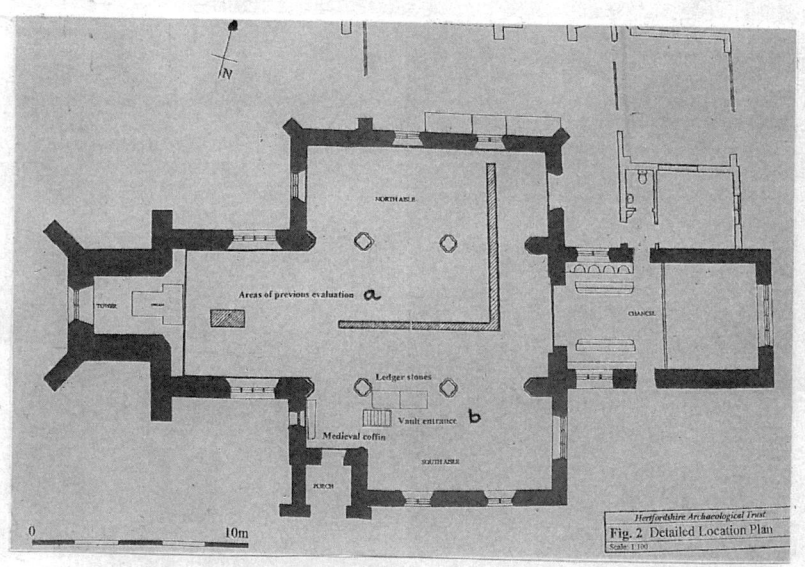

37. Plan of All Saints' Church, Milton.

(a) excavations in the nave (1999)   (b) examination of Knight's vault (2001)

© Hertfordshire Archaeological Trust (now Archaeological Solutions Ltd)

All Saints' Church, Milton

38. view from the southwest.

39. view from the south east.

All Saints' Church, Milton

40. view of Norman arch between the nave and the chancel.

41. font, medieval coffin lid fixed to wall next to the south porch entrance.

All Saints' Church, Milton

42. the south aisle (manorial chapel).

43. east window in the south aisle.

All Saints' Church, Milton

44. vault entrance, left: inside vault, right.

© Hertfordshire Archaeological Trust (now Archaeological Solutions)

45. Memorial monuments: Samuel Knight, died 1835 (south wall of south aisle), left; Rev Samuel Knight, died 1829 (west wall of south aisle), right; produced by Sir R Chantrey.

All Saints' Church, Milton

46. Memorial monument: Elizabeth Knight, died 1800 (south wall of south aisle), produced by Flaxman one of England's most famous sculptors.

47. Memorial monument: Rev Samuel Knight, died 1790 (south wall of south aisle), rector and lord of the manor.

All Saints' Church, Milton

48. view of the chancel ceiling which is a copy of that in the Roman Catholic Church in Cambridge by Pugin the notable 19th century architect.

All Saints' Church, Milton

49. Sedilia on the right hand side of the chancel, between this and the church banner is the piscina.

50. Misericords in the choir stalls on the left hand side of the chancel.

All Saints' Church, Milton

51. view of barrel roof in the nave.

52. view of the north aisle from the nave (note doors leading to the church hall).

All Saints' Church, Milton

53. view of the organ in front of the entrance to the tower.

54. Church annex (hall) built in the 1980's.

All Saints' Church, Milton

55. view of the Old Rectory built in 1846, now the 'Each' Hospice.

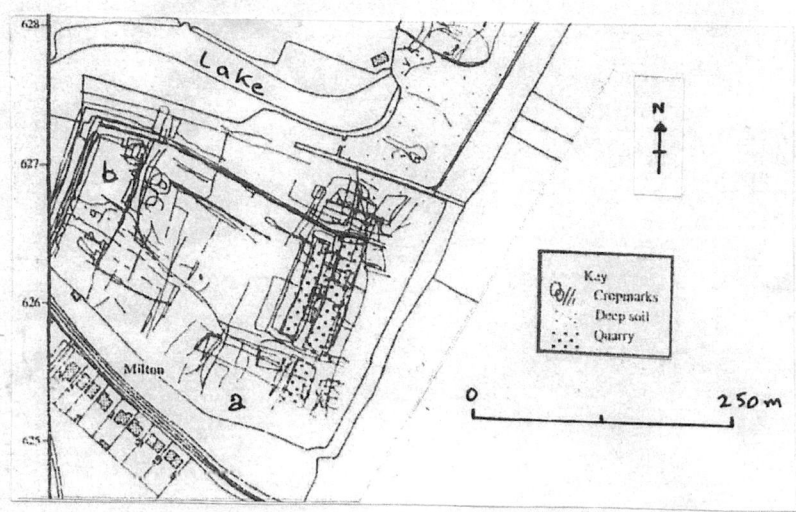

56. Crop marks at the left of Hill Close showing numerous features in the area of the proposed 13th century manor house (after Palmer in Robinson & Guttmann 1996).

(a) Hill Close   (b) site of 13th century manor house surrounded by features suggesting a moat.

57. View east across Hill Close. Note crop mark (dark green grass) for the moat feature running east and in the foreground, north-south.

58. Archaeology Rheesearch carrying out a magnetometry survey at Hill Close in 2007 on the site of the 13th century manor house.

59. Possible corner foundation stone found on the site of the 13th century manor house.

60. A medieval whetstone found on the site of the 13th century manor house.

61. Medieval Hedingham pottery rim sherd found on the site of the 13th century manor house.

62. Medieval jug handles found on the site of the 13th century manor house.

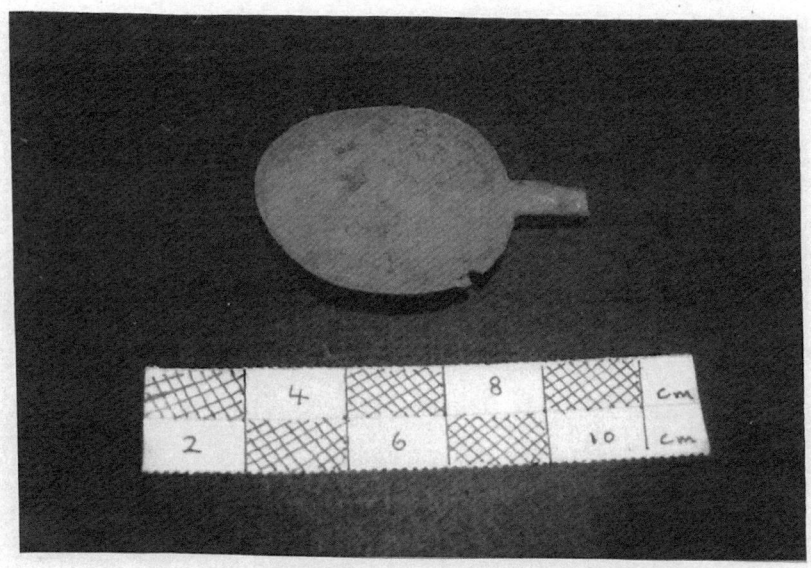

63. Medieval copper alloy spoon bowl found on the site of the 13th century manor house.

64. Medieval silver penny found at Hill Close, Milton (x 4.5).

65. Tudor red bricks of foundations revealed by Essex County Council archaeologists in 2013 adjacent to Milton Hall, are either the foundations of the Tudor manor house, or re-use for outbuildings of the present Hall.

66. Presence of stone with the Tudor bricks, suggest re-use from earlier buildings (13th century manor house or monastic buildings).

67. View down across the garden at the 'Each' Children's Hospice towards Milton brook which is in the tree boundary next to the remaining manorial fish pond. Note Goding Way in the background.

68. The last of the manorial fish ponds converted into a wild life pond next to Milton brook at the bottom of the garden at the 'Each' Children's Hospice.

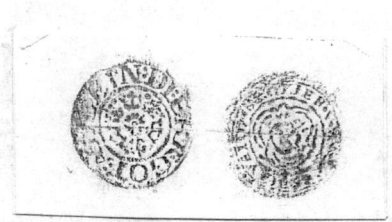

69. A pencil trace of a 17th century Nuremberg jetton found in a front garden at Fen Road, Milton. This ancient road brought people from afar via the River Cam to the village.
(with thanks to Douglas Brooklyn)

70. Another example of Milton's connection with Europe over 400 years ago – a Raeren stoneware drinking jug base (Rhineland) 1480-1550, also found in a garden at Fen Road, Milton.
(with thanks to Michael Waggett)

71. Front view of the present Milton Hall built in 1794 as the 3rd manor house replacing the 2nd manor house of Tudor origin.

72. Back view of the present Milton Hall.

73. The ha-ha (left of centre). A ditch boundary separating the rear garden of Milton Hall from the parkland acting as a deterrent with an associated wall or hedge to livestock from entering the garden.

74. East end of the Humphrey Repton lake showing the 'serpentine' curve. Photograph taken showing years of neglect before recent restoration.

75. North Lodge before restoration. Note elaborate patterns with the contrasting red and grey/white brickwork and the gate posts with gates. The chimney stacks appear to have been removed at an earlier date.

76. North Lodge gate with indistinct shield, possibly from the coat of arms of the Baumgartners, the last manorial family in residence at Milton Hall.

77. North Lodge gate posts before restoration. Note 'new' Ely Road constructed in the early 1960's through earlier Milton Hall parkland into the High Street at the junction with Fen Road.

78. A remaining part of the Milton Hall estate wall, opposite the College of West Anglia which ran from North Lodge to West Lodge. Note the patterns of red and grey/white bricks.

79. West Lodge at the junction of the High Street and Knights Way (on the earlier site of the road to Milton Hall). The lodge was restored many years ago, but two gate posts and part of the estate wall remain along the High Street.

80. The old milestone on the grass verge along the old Ely Road by the allotments north of North Lodge. Note 4 miles to Cambridge and 55 miles to London.

6. Land to the people

It was now November, and Tom was in the middle of his half term week's break from college, which included two Saturdays when he also had a break from his tutorials with Dr Crowfoot. Already, in the first half of the term, Tom had attended more than half of the tutorials in his course on the archaeology of Milton through time providing extra coaching for his local history project within his 'A' level archaeology course. Dr Crowfoot had covered the period of prehistory through to the end of the 18th century with the respective invasions and settlement of the Romans, Anglo-Saxons, Vikings and the Normans – the last of the major military invasions in our history. During this time, Milton had evolved into a significant village just 3 miles from the ancient university city of Cambridge.

Because Tom did not leave Milton during the half term break to take a holiday with his parents, this gave him time to consolidate his tutorial work so far, and as Dr Crowfoot had suggested earlier, to go with him to All Saints' Church and see the architectural features which he had described in his last tutorial before the half term break. Tom and Dr Crowfoot arranged to visit the church on the Thursday morning of the half term week when the church would be open for the lunch group. It was a bright, sunny morning, just right for taking a few photographs of the outside of the church. After Tom and Dr Crowfoot had walked round the outside of the church and noted those architectural features described in Dr Crowfoot's tutorial, they then entered the church through the south porch, and took note of the architecture and memorial monuments within the church.

After an hour or so, they left the church and Dr Crowfoot pointed out to Tom that Milton Hall, the last manor house in the village could be seen to the north of the church, through the trees now that most of the leaves had fallen; they then went out of the churchyard into the road. Directly opposite them was the new rectory, replacing the old rectory, built in 1846 which now had become the main building in the 'Each' children's hospice. This building could be clearly seen ahead of Tom and Dr Crowfoot as they turned left and walked towards the hospice grounds, such an appropriate tranquil setting with the house surrounded by a lawn, which in turn was protected by mature trees. As Tom and Dr Crowfoot returned back down Church Lane before dispersing to their respective homes, Dr Crowfoot said to Tom, " You are now passing two of the oldest thatched cottages in the village, the one on our right was extended in the 20th century." When tutor and student got to the corner of Church Lane with Fen Road, Dr Crowfoot had further words to say about two buildings, one immediately behind them, the other opposite them on Fen Road. "The public house, the Jolly Brewers behind us, is a 17th century building (initially timber framed), which was once a brewery belonging to the Essex family between the 1840's and 1925. Opposite us is another house, at least 17th century called Queen Ann Lodge; as you can see, there are some intriguing plaster reliefs on the outside of the house including lion heads and fruit. About 40 years ago the thatched roof was replaced with tiles."

"Well Tom, our excursion today, primarily to see the church architecture, has come to an end. But, in my tutorial the Saturday after next, we will take up our story of the development of Milton through time as we enter the 19th century, looking at the significance of the Enclosure Act for Milton as I mentioned at the end of our last tutorial. We will also note the buildings that existed in the village at the time of the Enclosure Act for Milton in 1802, some of these we have seen today, and see what other types of house were built in the 19th century and still with us. For now, I will say Goodbye, and see you in just over a week's time – enjoy the rest of your half term break!" "Goodbye," said Tom, "and thank you for such an informative excursion this morning, I look forward to seeing more of these large artefacts, such as buildings, they are just as interesting as those smaller objects made by the human hand – tools, pottery and coins."

Half term seemed all too short for Tom, he was now back at college and the first week of the remaining part of the autumn term had equally flashed by; it was Saturday morning again, and Tom's first visit for three weeks to Kiln Cottage for another tutorial with Dr Crowfoot. This Saturday morning was a typical dull, damp and cold November day, as usual Tom could not wait to absorb the homely comforts of Kiln Cottage – the comfortable chair by the warm log fire, the biscuits and coffee, somehow having a flavour more appealing than in a student cafe. Tom having gone through this calming ritual after his arrival at Kiln Cottage, heard Dr Crowfoot searching around in the dusty cupboard under the stairs, then there was a pause, before Dr Crowfoot entered the room with an armful of maps.

" As you know Tom, today we are going to look at the Enclosure Act and what it meant for the continuing development of Milton to modern times, these maps will be useful." With these words, Dr Crowfoot settled into his fireside chair opposite Tom and began his tutorial. "You will recall Tom in our last tutorial, we discussed the medieval fields in Milton which were established by the 14th century and described as open fields. There were three main fields occupying around 1120 acres. The other major block of land of just over 500 acres by 1600, belonged to the manor. In many villages, by the 16th century there was often extensive enclosure of land by the more ruthless lords of the manor, particularly where there were few tenants; a notable example of this was at Bray's manor, Landbeach. Here a new lord of the manor, Richard Kirby from London, fixed such high rents which the small number of tenants could not afford, that their houses were abandoned. As sheep farming was increasing at that time, the abandoned homesteads disappeared being replaced by grass suitable for grazing sheep, giving rise to a subsequent good source of income for the manor; the platforms of the abandoned cottages can still be seen as elevations in the pasture land at Wort's meadow."

Enclosure Act

Dr Crowfoot continued, "By the 18th century, it was realized that the injustices of earlier land divisions often by lords of the manor and the deleterious effect it had on the village folk, could not continue and an Act of Parliament was passed towards rectifying the problem. Some of the first Enclosure awards took place in the fens as early as 1750 onwards." Tom then interrupted, "I know Milton has fenland near the River Cam, but what was happening with the land division nearer the village?" "I was just coming to that after considering what was happening on a wider scale," said Dr Crowfoot, he continued. "In 1794, a Charles Vancouver published a 'General View of the Agriculture of the County of Cambridgeshire', for the Board of Agriculture. Vancouver estimated that of 147,000 acres of arable land in Cambridgeshire, 132,000 acres was still in common fields. Vancouver stated that it was indispensably necessary to enclose the land into smaller packages. This led to a flood of applications. Between 1796 and 1850, ninety five parishes in upland Cambridgeshire were enclosed by Act of Parliament, four by private agreement. This involved about 160,000 acres of former common fields and open pasture lands. The Enclosure Act brought about a significant change in the landscape – in a sense another artefact of mankind's making. A large medieval open field was divided into small geometrical fields, often rectangular, associated with a farmstead, although remnants of the earlier common field boundaries can be seen as thicker hedge and tree boundaries; we will consider this further when we look at specific fields in Milton. Enclosure sometimes led to roads being straightened to run along the geometric alignment of enclosed fields."

Dr Crowfoot then explained to Tom that dividing the land into smaller plots was not simply a matter of defining a field boundary by hedgerows, ditches and roads. A major cost involved was often erecting fences and painting them, planting new hedges along the new boundaries, blocking up old drainage ditches while constructing new ditches with brick and timber bridges placed across them for access to neighbouring land; gates were also needed. With the establishment of the new Enclosure plots of land, new farmsteads were built to farm a prescribed area of land, whether purchased by a freeholder or provided by the manor to a copyholder. Where these new farms arose near the centre of a village, the landscape of the village soon changed dramatically, due not only to the farm buildings adding to the number of houses in the village, but also to other houses as the population increased with people having a wider range of occupations ranging from increased farm workers to supportive trades associated with the land and the domestic scene. In some instances, the change in the landscape of a village with the need for more housing, led to a reduction or the loss of traditional village greens. By the 1880's, the rural landscape of Cambridgeshire was similar to today in many areas.

Enclosure Award for Milton

"Tom," Dr Crowfoot exclaimed, "we will now look at the Enclosure Act as it applied to Milton. In 1800, the lord of the manor Samuel Knight, and the rector obtained without opposition, an Enclosure Act award which was executed on 8th July 1802. During the rest of that year and for some time after this, the division of the parish land into smaller allotments was instigated. The award dealt with 1110 acres, and 217 acres of ancient closes which included 74 acres around Milton Hall. Samuel Knight had 487 acres, the rector and vicar 260 acres, and two Cambridge colleges with around 90 acres between them. Knight's allotments were in the northern half of Milton with 300 acres in the east, and 85 acres in the west; later this became New Close farm next to Rectory farm with 200 acres. A further 115 acres of allotments by the northern boundary of the parish went to Waterbeach landowners, leading to the irregular parish boundary existing today associated with the non-alignment of field boundaries. There was a remainder of 104 acres for freehold. There were also five owners having 30-60 acres each within 210 acres, while there were seven others with 16-20 acres each; eleven smallholders had a total of 34 acres. By 1820, there were 10 main farmers with a few occupying over 100 acres, and by the 1850's the Knight's estate had increased to 568 acres, of which 345 acres was arable and about 150 acres grassland. In 1836, a five course rotation of cultivation was in operation on 215 acres at Manor farm, 180 acres of arable northeast of the village, and one of about 145 acres from a farmstead at Fen End; this is the area to the south of Fen Road, where there were a number of farmsteads with land where the Country Park is today; there were also two smaller farms covering an area of 47 acres."

Enclosure at Fen End

"Now Tom, I would like to expand on the significance of the area of Fen End," Dr Crowfoot continued. "This is where Kiln Cottage is and the division of the land here at Enclosure, provides a good example of the way a large medieval open field, in this case Backsbite (later Baitsbite) field was divided up at Enclosure." At this point, Dr Crowfoot selected out one of the maps he had recovered from the cupboard under the stairs. "Tom, let's put this copy of the Enclosure Award map for Milton in 1802, on the table here by the window, I will hold one side down, you the other." Tom was amazed at how different the village looked in 1802. "So few houses Dr Crowfoot, but many mostly rectangular shaped fields extending from houses along the roads into the earlier medieval open fields," said Tom. "Yes Tom, that is the significance of the Enclosure Act, more land to the people," Dr Crowfoot replied, and continued. "This is clearly shown south of Fen Road in the area of Fen End where there were a number of farmsteads including Milton House (the home of William Cole the antiquarian), each with plots of land running in a southerly direction through what was Baitsbite field and now the site of the Country Park.

Today when we take a walk around the Park, we can see remnants of the old field boundaries established following the Enclosure Act being implemented. For example, when you enter the Country Park from the Old School Lane cul-de-sac, you enter land that once belonged to King's College together with Cole's house, most of this plot in the Park was excavated for sand and gravel in the 20th century, and the gravel pit which arose, is known as Todd's pit, but more about this next week. Quickly turning left, we enter another plot of land which leads into the central part of the Park where at its southern end there is the small pond with a 'Monet' bridge, a spot where children enjoy pond-dipping; this pond is the remaining part of a filled in gravel pit and is called 'Hall's pool after the farming family who lived in a house at Fen End and farmed the land, all the way from Fen Road to the 13th public drain near the visitor centre during the first half of the 20th century. Either side of this central part of the Park, at its western boundary with Todd's pit, and at its eastern boundary with the largest gravel pit area known as Dickerson's pit, there are distinct raised banks running along the position of the Enclosure field boundaries. Here Tom we have an example of landscape archaeology, the more so as planted on these banks are essentially two species of trees, one large, the oak, the other smaller and less contained, the hawthorn. You will note that there are only a few oaks separating rows of hawthorn, the latter having invaded over the last 50 years or so, the land that was once pasture land for cattle and seen today as dense hawthorn copses in the Park. This association of primarily two species of tree planted along an Enclosure boundary, is in keeping with the date of Enclosure according to the studies of a Dr Hooper who demonstrated that the further you go back in time, there is the likelihood of there being more tree species along an old field boundary if they have not been cleared. Although some of the oaks do not appear too large for something less than 200 years, many of the hawthorn trees can be seen to be very old with their thick twisted trunks."

Population distribution

"Let us return to the map of the Enclosure award for Milton," Dr Crowfoot continued. "You can clearly see Tom that most of the houses in the village were concentrated along the High Street and Fen Road, with a few along Butt Lane, and many were associated with the geometrical plots of land allocated at Enclosure; the smallest plots for smallholders, larger plots for small farmers, often keeping cows for milk, and the largest plots of land for grazing sheep or for arable crops, farmed by the main farmers. One of these was Manor farm (the site of the farm house is where the College of West Anglia is today – more locally known as the Farm School).

Following Enclosure, several farmers who had been tenant farmers, particularly of the manor as copyholders, gradually improved their income over outgoings, to the extent that they were able to buy land and increasingly therefore became significant freeholders; one of these farming families was the Gunnells. A Thomas Gunnell who rented both Manor and Rectory farms in 1861, occupying 570 acres, made a reputation for breeding long-woolled Lincoln sheep, which led to annual sales of these prize winning sheep at Rectory farm until the 1880's. Thomas Gunnell also bred turkeys, bulls and heifers. The other prominent farmer in the village was Alfred Marshall Robinson of Benet Farm, south of the village; he was farming 400 acres by 1876 and specialized in producing Hampshire Down sheep."

Houses and architecture

"At this point in our tutorial Tom, it is interesting to take a look at some of the houses shown mostly as rectangular or 'T' shaped blocks on the Enclosure map, some of which are still standing today." Dr Crowfoot took a deep breath and continued, "the occupants of many of these houses would have been involved with the land. We have noted the smaller dwellings on Fen Road, at Fen End were small farms of the manor with land now part of the Country Park. However, there was one exception here, Milton or Cole's house which was once a 17th century farmhouse belonging to King's College. We mentioned this property earlier with reference to the notable antiquarian William Cole who lived here in the late 18th century. William Cole came to Milton in 1768 when he took up his post as curate at Waterbeach church, and embarked on 'modernising' the King's farmhouse over the next few years with architectural features typical of a late 18th century house. These included installing bay windows at the rear and east end with small paned sash windows, and corridors along the north side of the ground floor and first floor. Many of the clear glass window panes, were replaced with stained glass depicting heraldic motives; these were acquired from other buildings being renovated, such as large mansions belonging to titled people, churches and university colleges. When Cole died in 1782, his Will stated that the stained glass be removed and auctioned off, unfortunately we do not know where and to whom the glass went. The house was extended westwards by W Dunn an antiques dealer in the 1920's. Opposite Cole's house on the north side of Fen Road was a large farm at Enclosure, noted for its association with the Goodin family; this was the only farm on this side of the road and it was demolished in the first part of the 20th century.

Other, distinctive but smaller houses in the village built in the 17th or 18th century and present at Enclosure, were a group of thatched farm workers' cottages, now one property opposite Hill Close in Fen Road, and another similar situation of a cluster of working cottages with a tiled roof, becoming one, as seen today on the right hand side and end on to the High Street beyond the Waggon & Horses public house. Another small cottage is to be found away from the road, further towards the centre of the village on the right of the High Street in the direction of Cambridge, opposite the cluster of shops and bus stop after we have passed the two public houses, the Lion & Lamb (brick overlaying a timber frame), and The White Horse which were also present at Enclosure. Returning to the area of the junction between the High Street and Fen Road, at Enclosure there was the village pond (filled in, during the 1930's) where now is the entrance to Willow Crescent. This mid-20th century housing development takes the name Willow from the mid-19th century large farmhouse, Willow House, which stood on the right hand side at the entrance to Willow Crescent and was associated with a terrace of grey brick cottages nearby, which were end on to the pond and High Street; these cottages present at Enclosure, also became one property which today offers bed and breakfast accommodation. The Willow farm complex was occupied by members of the Gunnell family in the 19th century, and the site of the pond is called Pond Green where our late 20th century village sign has been placed.

It is worth noting Tom, that one architectural feature which often indicates that a house is 17th century or earlier, is the presence of the main chimney stack at the centre of the property; this reflects the fact that back in history before chimneys were built, the smoke from a centrally placed fire in an open room, just vented to the outside via a hole in the roof! Our 17th century chimneys usually had fire places placed back to back for the adjacent rooms on one or more floors, providing 'centralised' heating within the house. But later in the 18th and 19th centuries, fire places and hence chimney stacks were often placed at the gable ends of the properties for the rooms to the left and right of the central main front door, leading to the disadvantage of greater heat loss to the outside. Before leaving the topic of properties present in Milton at the time of Enclosure, we finally return to Church Lane where in addition to the thatched cottages we noted when we walked down Church Lane after visiting the church, there were other thatched cottages here (where now there are bungalows), until the early 20th century. It is important to note that these thatched cottages and

Cole's house, were timber framed with lath and plaster walls, sometimes with inserts of clunch and brickwork."

At this point in the tutorial, it was now Tom's cue to pose a question to Dr Crowfoot. "It has been fascinating," said Tom, "to become aware of what the Enclosure Act meant for changing the landscape of Milton, and in turn, the increase in more independent farming families whose houses are still with us today. But, the population must also have been increasing steadily through the 19th century. Is the evidence for this, the other houses in the village which were built of blue-grey bricks with slate roofs and are seen along the main roads in the village today?" "Correct Tom, and to illustrate this further, let us refer to one of the other maps we have here," said Dr Crowfoot. "This Ordnance Survey map of 1887 shows exactly what you concluded. We can see many more houses have appeared along the High Street, Fen Road and Butt Lane in between the older houses we have discussed that were present at Enclosure. These additional houses built of blue-grey, gault clay bricks with slate roofs, were built on plots, some of which may have had earlier cottages built there, but were either destroyed by fire (there was that devastating fire in the village in 1735), or had deteriorated beyond economic repair. Towards the end of the century and into the 20th century, a few houses were being built of a better quality, cream-coloured brick made in Cambridge or at Burwell – known as 'whites'. Houses constructed of these bricks, sometimes had horizontal courses of contrasting dark red bricks built into the brick courses, as well as red brick lintels over the windows. Examples of this can be seen at a house on the Landbeach Road in Milton, and the farmhouse once occupied by Ephraim Halls and his family on Fen Road who farmed the land to the rear which is now in the centre of the Country Park where 'Halls' pool exists, as I mentioned earlier. Incidently, the Halls house was built in the early 20th century on the site of an earlier farmhouse present at Enclosure and was a copyhold farm of the manor until the 20th century, but more about this later."

"As we have become aware Tom," Dr Crowfoot continued, "we have noted the increase in houses in the village after Enclosure in 1802, and we now need to relate this expansion in property, to the increase in population with some figures. The population of Milton in 1800 was 270, but by 1831 it had increased by over a 100 to 377, then increased by about 90 in each decade for the next two decades, before dropping by a tenth in 1861, and increasing again to 576 in 1871. Therefore Tom, the increase in properties seen on the 1887 Ordnance Survey map by comparison with those seen on the Enclosure Award map, is in keeping with the increase in population.

Other distinctive houses and land holdings

By the mid-19th century, the farms in the parish had consolidated into the three largest farms covering 940 acres in 1861 with other land occupied by two farms of 135 acres and one of 70 acres. There were five or six smallholders with 10-40 acres each, one of these was the farm at Fen End operated by the Gunnell family as a copyhold farm of the manor, later to be farmed by Ephraim Halls in the 20th century as mentioned earlier. In 1890, the rector let 12 acres of land off Butt Lane for use as allotments (this land more recently became part of the land for the Milton Park and Ride site). It was during this time that the larger grey brick farm houses were built in the village i.e. Shirley Lodge on Fen Road (at the later junction of Fen Road and a late 20th century housing development known as Shirley Close; this house was demolished and replaced by maisonettes in the 1980's). Another large Victorian house associated with The Vineries Nursery, was built on the Cambridge Road opposite the present junction of this road with Coles Road, and was occupied by the Walkling family for many years. Other double depth houses were built as private dwellings around the village at this time, notably along the High Street which today have become partly converted for commercial use."

"Before we leave the subject of buildings in Milton built during the 19th century, there are some properties worthy of note, of wider significance," remarked Dr Crowfoot. "We return again to Milton Hall. Two entrances were established to the Hall, each with a lodge, one from the High Street cutting across the parkland at the front of the house, the other was at the north end of the grounds opposite the junction of the Ely Road with its connecting road to the Landbeach Road; the location of these lodges can be clearly seen on our 1887 Ordnance Survey map. In both instances, the lodges were built with gates, the High street entrance became known as the West Lodge, the other, the North Lodge. These lodges (still present today), were built of blue-grey bricks(North Lodge and white bricks West Lodge) with inserted courses of red bricks around the doors, windows and corners of the walls; the roofs were of slate. There was a wall around part of the Milton Hall estate, which included a connection between the two lodges. This wall was also built of blue-grey bricks with patterning by red brick insertions; a significant length of this wall still exists, running from West Lodge to North Lodge along the back of the gardens of Knight's Way opposite the Farm School's main entrance, with disconnections for the entrance of Knight's Way next to West Lodge, and the Ely Road next to North Lodge.

Other buildings erected were in the public domain. We have already referred to the rectory built in 1846, but 10 years before this, the village national school was built in Fen Road on land next to the present entrance to the housing cul-de-sac of Hall End (it was demolished in the late 1960's, almost 10 years after the new school in Butt Lane was opened). The building of the school was funded by King's College with an associated school house for the caretaker. The only other church in Milton other than All Saints' parish church, was built in 1865 for the Baptists and is situated on the High Street (it remained as such until recently when it became one of the Worldwide New Apostolic Church centres). Between 1841 and the late 1880's, Milton House where William Cole lived in the 18th century, became a private school for boys and girls."

Lord of the manor ceases residence, land is sold

"We are nearing the end of this morning's tutorial Tom, and I wish to return to the status of the manor of Milton with its residence being Milton Hall. How long could the manor survive after Enclosure with its effects on landownership and associated changes in the landscape, population and occupations?" This question, Dr Crowfoot put to Tom. "Well Dr Crowfoot," Tom replied. "I am aware that there is no lord of the manor today, and probably not for many years since the 19th century. I would be grateful if you could enlighten me on this perception, perhaps it is nearly right?" "Again Tom, your intuition is on the right lines," Dr Crowfoot assured Tom. "The last resident lord of the manor at Milton Hall was John Percy Baumgartner who became heavily mortgaged such that in 1862 he was compelled to sell the Hall with 73 acres of land to Richard Miller, a wine merchant in Cambridge. He was followed by the Rev Dr Charles William Giles between 1866 until his death in 1888; he in turn was succeeded by the Pryors of Cambridge from 1889, then others into the 20th century. After selling the Hall and land, John Baumgartner maintained his manorial rights until he died in 1903 when his two daughters inherited such rights until 1930 – this will be discussed further in our next tutorial. Estate lands, Manor farm (96 acres) and New Close farm (92 acres), were sold after 1862 to a succession of people. In 1908, Manor farm with 261 acres, and a further 78 acres in 1910 with New Close farm in 1912, went to the Cambridgeshire County Council. Further land purchases to the 1970's, resulted in the County Council owning 455 acres mostly north and west of the village, let to smallholders; the County Council becoming the largest landowner in the parish.

Occupations

"Finally Tom," Dr Crowfoot said with a welcomed tone, "we will take a brief look at some of the occupations in the village in the 19th century, and become aware of some of the family names associated with these trades, still found in Milton today. Arable farming remained at the forefront of farming followed by sheep farming which was beginning to decline towards the end of the century. On the other hand, dairy farming increased, an occupation that was undertaken on many smaller farms, and this was associated with an increase in pasture land from around 250 acres in 1880, to over 500 acres at the beginning of the 20th century. Earlier, I mentioned the building of some large Victorian houses in the village, one of these on the right of the Cambridge Road going in the direction of Cambridge was called The Vineries. This house was associated with nurseries producing salad crops and cut flowers from the 1880's for distribution beyond Cambridge; the efficient production of these horticultural products was brought about by the construction of many greenhouses, and later The Vineries became the Alexandra Nurseries with the Walkling family being involved over many years into the 20th century.

Many smallholders were involved with market gardening from the mid-19th century covering over 21 acres by 1895; vegetables, fruit and flowers were grown and predominant families were the Coulsons, Pearsons and Easys (members of the latter family were also involved in dairy farming). Other occupations necessary for any village community, were butchers, bakers, grocers, general store, blacksmiths (there was one near the junction of the High Street and Fen Road), wheelright, tailors, shoemakers, saddlers, and cycle agents. Some of the main families involved with these occupations were in addition to those already mentioned, Day, Burling, Kidman, Starling, Wilson, Butler, Wilkin, Flack, Froment, Butcher and Robinson. A small building business run by the Unwins, appeared in the village from 1850 and were responsible for building some of the houses in the village into the beginning of the 20th century.

There remains one final occupation to comment on where only a small number of men from Milton were involved Tom, and that was coprolite digging." Tom looked bemused, "Coprolites! What are they," said Tom. "You may well ask Tom," replied Dr Crowfoot with a whimsical smile. "Too many people think that coprolites are the fossilized remains of dinosaur dung, but this is only a minor source of the material. Most coprolites were formed from decaying molluscs and other sea creatures that have become fossilized since the Cretaceaous period over 100 million years ago, and they are found in Cambridgeshire within greensand at the bottom layer of chalk overlying gault clay running in a line at the northern edge of the chalk land from southwest to northeast, roughly from Abington to Soham; the richest sources are on the other side of the River Cam from Milton, at Fen Ditton, Horningsea through to Burwell. But, why the interest in coprolites?" Tom thought that they may have something to do with the building trade, but before he had time to make this inaccurate comment, Dr Crowfoot continued, "With arable farming being so prevalent in Cambridgeshire, including Milton, it was discovered that coprolites being rich in phosphates, were an excellent source of these substances for an important chemical fertilizer. It was the Cambridge scientist Professor J S Henslow who realized the potential of coprolites for a fertilizer. This resulted in the world's first industry for obtaining a chemical fertilizer from nature, being established in Cambridgeshire from the mid-19th century. The coprolites were dug from pits, often several feet down, before being ground down to a powder by various types of mill, after transportation via road, lode and river. However, Milton played a very minor role in providing coprolites compared with the rich sources beneath the chalk east of the River Cam. There were no coprolite diggers in Milton in 1871 and only four in 1881 when the industry was at its peak; by 1887 the small coprolite works in Milton had closed down. But, as major works were only across the river, several men living in Milton went to work in the coprolite pits at Horningsea, Stow-cum-Quy and Bottisham because the wages for a coprolite digger were over four times that of a standard farm labourer's wage (7-8 shillings a week); the high wages were due to the fact that a peak tonnage of fertilizer of 250 tons a year was worth over half a million pounds. This brought about an increase in the population of Cambridgeshire villages within 3-4 miles of coprolite mines (73 out of 145 villages between 1870 and 1880). However, with cheap imports of coprolite derived fertilizer being imported from the USA at the end of the 19th century, our industry declined to a minimum by the beginning of the 20th century.

From an archaeological aspect, aerial views of fields today reveal the outline of coprolite pits, but even more impressive are the deeper pits naturalized as ponds that can be seen at Stow-cum-Quy Fen. These pits can be reached by a relatively easy walk from Milton across Milton Fen and over Baitsbite lock to Horningsea.

Milton Fen was also subjected to land division at Enclosure. This included the construction of Bank (later Bankers) Ditch running north-south for over a mile, and the erection of a windpump to pump water from the Ditch to the River Cam. The pump was removed in 1841, so that the railway track for the Cambridge to Ely line operated by the Eastern Counties Railway Company could be put in place. It was this company which compensated the parish for the loss of land with £50 and the money was used to place a clock in the tower of All Saints' Church as mentioned in Chapter 5.

Finally Tom, in this and the previous week's tutorial, I have referred to a number of distinctive, existing buildings in Milton. Notably, these are All Saints' Church, Milton Hall, Cole's House and public houses such the Jolly Brewers. These properties are designated Grade II listed buildings which means that any restoration work or extensions, has to be carried out with due regard for the preservation of the period character of these buildings. Some of the 17th and 18th century cottages in the village are also listed, as are the 19th century North and West Lodges of Milton Hall. Furthermore, much of the land associated with Milton Hall, an area around the junction of the High Street, Fen Road, the Ely Road and Church Lane, the Jolly Brewers and cottages on the north side of Fen Road, and on the south side of Fen Road – Cole's (Milton) House and the Halls old farm house, are all conservation areas. Away from the village, an area around Baits Bite Lock including the old lock keeper's cottage, is also a conservation area."

"The tutorial for today has now come to an end Tom," Dr Crowfoot concluded. " But, when you have a spare moment and you want to get out of the house away from your book work, take a walk back to the churchyard at All Saints' Church, and go to the far end nearest the road into the hospice, there you will see under the trees where the churchyard is rather over grown with weeds, three distinctive graves. One the Robinson's has a large monument, the second with an iron chain surround for the Rev Dr Charles William Giles and the third a cluster of graves for members of the Gunnell family. The people of Milton buried here are a memorial in themselves of lives lived through that great period of social change in the village in the 19th century following the Enclosure Act award for Milton."

> *"No man but feels more of a man in the world*
> *if he have but a bit of ground that can he can*
> *call his own. However small it is on the*
> *surface, it is four thousand miles deep,*
> *and that is a very handsome property."*
>
> Charles Dudley Warner (1829-1900)

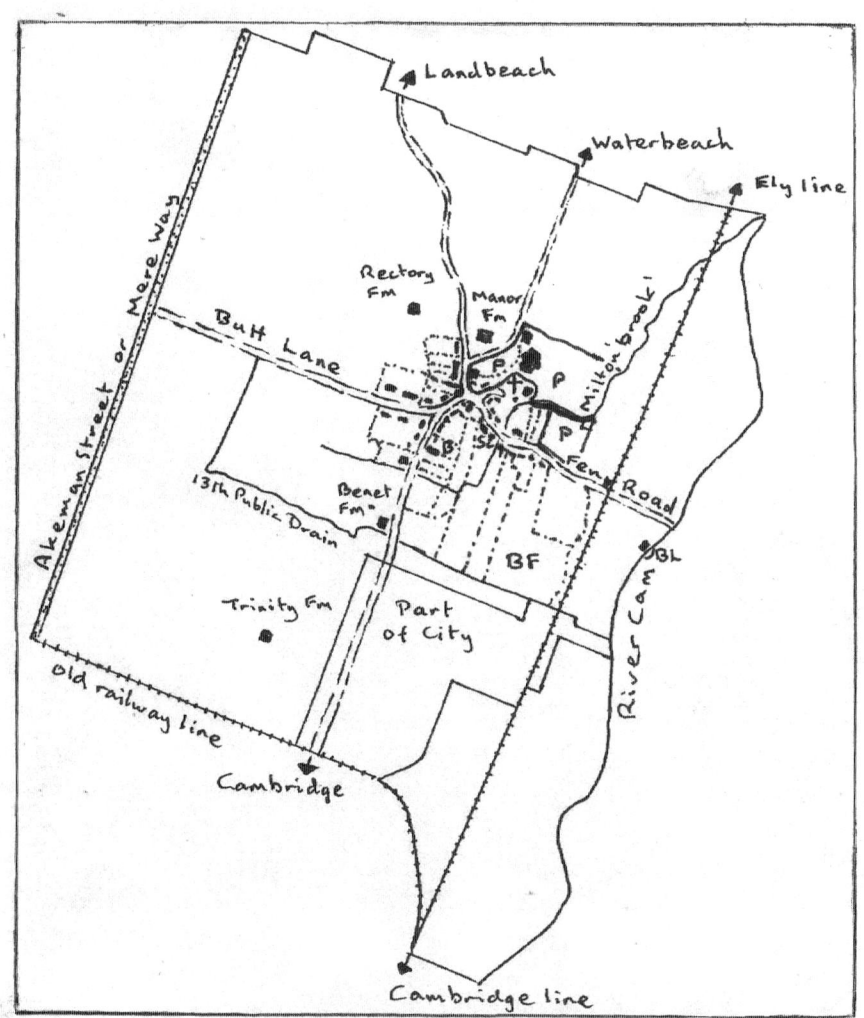

81. Sketch map of post-Enclosure Milton Village, 1802 to 1900.

BF previously Baitsbite Field   BL Baitsbite lock   P parkland in Milton Hall

—·—·— Enclosure boundaries   ▊▄ buildings at centre of village   Sc school

✝ All Saints' Church   B Baptist Chapel   ▆ ▪ ▪ Milton Hall with two lodges

82. View from All Saints' Church tower (early 20th century) showing Church Lane with its 17th and 18th century thatched cottages, rear of the Jolly Brewers (centre left) opposite Queen Ann Lodge on Fen Road (partly concealed by Poplar tree), the blacksmith's (centre right) at the junction of Fen Road with the High Street, and Willow Farmhouse can be seen through the trees (top right).

(Cambridgeshire Collection, with permission)

83. Enclosure bank between previously the Halls land and Dickerson's gravel pit in Milton Country Park. Note old hawthorn trees, and oak tree (left of centre), typical of an Enclosure boundary over 200 years ago.

84. Hawthorn trees established on previous meadow land. These trees arose from seeds of the hawthorn trees on the Enclosure bank, an example of re-naturalization of open land with trees and shrubs.

85. Old properties in Fen Road in the early 20th century. Goodin Farm (left), Shirley Lodge (centre), thatched cottage (centre right) and Halls Farm (right behind tree trunk). Apart from Halls Farm, all the other houses are 18th and 19th century and were demolished in the 20th century.

(Cambridgeshire Collection with permission)

86. A group of thatched cottages opposite Hill Close in Fen Road present at Enclosure in 1802, but now one property.

87. Recent photograph of the Halls Farmhouse built of Burwell white brick and contrasting red brick lintels and lines. This house built in 1910, replaced a late 18th century copyhold farmhouse. Note a barn annex has replaced the thatched cottage seen in illustration 85, and is attached to an 18th century cottage with a mansard roof (left).

(a)

(b)

88. (a) Halls farmhouse next to Cole's House (17th century), (centre). A white brick 19th century farmhouse (now flats), is at the extreme right.
(b) East end of Cole's House as seen from the garden of the previous Halls farm.

(a) (b)

89. (a) North annexe of Coles's House. Note inset stone heads probably acquired by William Cole from a church, abbey or college.
(b) Baptist Church in the High Street built 1865, now one of the Worldwide New Apostolic Church centres.

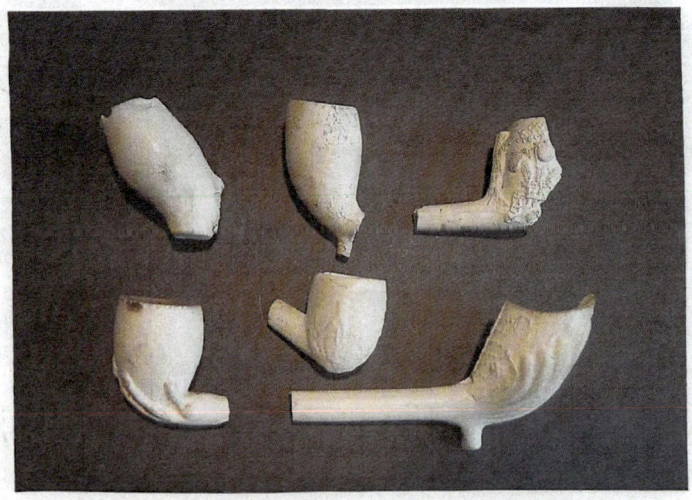

90. Bowls (or part) of clay pipes found in gardens, fields and allotments in Milton, dated 17th (top left) to 19th century. Note makers initial J on spur (top row, middle), and C (probably the Cleaver family, pipemakers of Cambridge 19th century), on bowl (bottom right).

These pipes reflect the last century of extensive farm workers on the land in Milton.

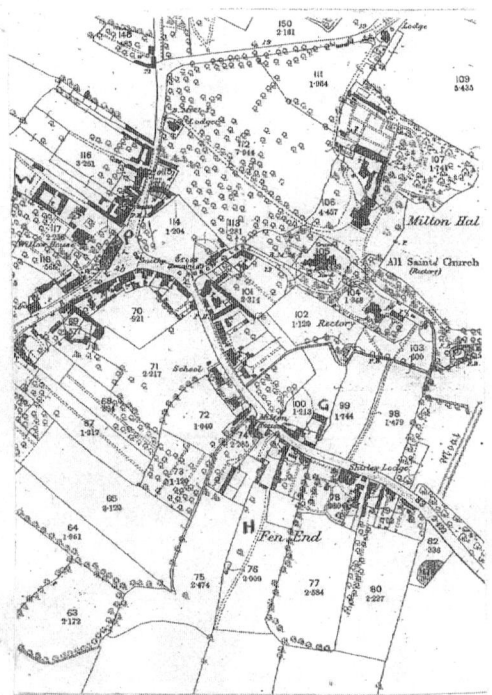

91. O.S. Cambridgeshire Sheet XL7 (1887) shows the location of houses with plots of land at the centre of Milton at the end of the 19th century.
Note: G, Goodin Farm; H, Halls Farm; Milton House (Cole's House) in Fen Road, and W, Willow Farm next to P, the village pond off the High Street. Also the *Moat* at Hill Close (extreme right of map).

(Cambridge Record Office, with permission)

7. Farmstead to suburbia

Another week had gone by, and the half term break seemed to be retreating fast into the past, as Tom had completed a further week of classes at his 6th form college in Cambridge. Saturday morning was here again with only one more tutorial for Tom to receive from Dr Crowfoot on the development of his village Milton. This morning's tutorial was going to bring Milton's past right up to the present day – a time when Tom was born at the end of the 20th century, and now, as a 6th form student, he had entered the 21st century. From now on, Tom was going to become even more aware of history in the making as Dr Crowfoot provided him with knowledge about the considerable changes that had occurred in the landscape of Milton in the last 100 years; these changes were already apparent by the time Tom was born. The village had evolved from being almost exclusively a farming community to one that was now almost urban, in fact, a suburban development on the outskirts of the city of Cambridge.

Tom was already aware that Milton as he saw it today, must have arisen through recent and rapid changes. It was with these thoughts in mind that Tom gave his usual, but this time, more positive three knocks on Dr Crowfoot's front door before being greeted by Dr Crowfoot, Caesar the cat rubbing his ankles and the smell of the welcoming refreshments being prepared by Mrs Crowfoot in the kitchen, welded to the back of Kiln Cottage. After these preliminaries, and both tutor and student settled in their respective chairs by the log fire, Dr Crowfoot launched straight into his last tutorial on the development of Milton observed primarily from an archaeological, architectural, landscape and socio-economic perspective.

"This morning Tom, we will continue our passage through time to arrive in a Milton as we see it today," these were the words that Dr Crowfoot uttered to Tom, as a relaxed smile of satisfaction with the near completion of his tutorials became evident. "Last Saturday Tom, we got to the end of the 19th century with the land having been divided up after Enclosure to accommodate a maximum number of farming families. Today we leave the 19th century and enter the 20th century which brought to Milton the greatest changes in its history. Technology and two world wars changed the face of the village from a small farming based village to a suburban complex embracing industry ranging from gravel extraction, to science based innovations, I like to sum up this phenomenon for Milton as, 'from farmstead to suburbia', so let us begin".

Population changes

"As we enter the 20th century, there had been a decline in the population of Milton from 576 in 1871, to 471 in 1901. This may have been in part, due to a succession of bad harvests in the late 19th century because of unseasonable weather, which resulted in people leaving the village to take up more urban occupations in nearby Cambridge. This phenomenon had been going on for decades, associated with the industrial revolution of the 18th and 19th centuries with people moving from rural areas to towns and cities throughout Britain. However, as we shall see later with commuting by rail and roads becoming more widespread in the second half of the 20th century, there was a reversal of this trend with people seeking less expensive housing in suburbia and in villages".

Already Tom was looking confused. He could see that since he was born, Milton had expanded in population with new housing developments, but with a fall in population a 100 years ago, why did the population recover and expand again then? Tom put this question to Dr Crowfoot, whereupon Dr Crowfoot replied, "in 1910 Tom, the population was still primarily concentrated along the High Street and Fen Road. But in 1911, 75 people were added to the parish from the north part of Chesterton which became joined to Milton parish. From then on, apart from the sad loss of several men from the village during the First World War, the population of Milton steadily increased to over 700 until the 1950's, and then increased to 850 by 1961. It is pertinent to comment here, on the erection of the War Memorial in the village soon after the First World War, which includes the names of those men of Milton who were lost during this war, then more names, but fortunately fewer, were added after the Second World War. The memorial first stood at the junction of the High Street with Fen Road, before being moved later in 1963, round the corner to the grassy area at the end of Cole's Road near its junction with Fen Road, I will refer to this again later when we deal with new roads."

"This was the beginning of the dramatic rise in the population of Milton," Dr Crowfoot continued, "which was destined to double, and then treble in the next four decades, as families moved out of Cambridge city and from further away, into Milton. This led to a change in the character of Milton from a hitherto farming community to a suburban complex, and was the reversal of population movement I mentioned earlier. But, apart from the less expensive houses in Milton compared with city prices and improved roads from the village, there were other reasons why people moved to live in Milton. These reasons we will deal with in turn, as the landscape of Milton changed during the 20th century due to the impact of industry, some occupying earlier farmland."

Landscape changes, agriculture declines

Dr Crowfoot continued, "let us take a look at Milton at the beginning of the transition period from farming to more urban industrial activity in the village. The first 50 years of the 20th century saw the final changes in farming in Milton. Cambridgeshire County Council acquired 430 acres of land between 1908 and 1912, which were divided into smallholdings. By 1915, there were 49 occupiers with 5 acres or less land, which diminished to 36 occupiers with under 20 acres by 1925; the farming family, the Halls in Fen Road were one of these. In the 1930's, 15 men farmed less than 100 acres with only 3-5 men farming more than that. The number of farm labourers fell from 100 in the early 1950's, to only 10 by 1980, with 12 working farms occupying the remaining farmland of 1125 acres north of the village. An important factor which led to the decline in farm labourers, was the advent of mechanisation on farms, notably tractors replacing horses and increasingly more sophisticated harvesting equipment – this automation reduced the need for manual labour.

There was also a change in the production of arable crops and farm animals in the final days of Milton being predominantly a farming village. The production of sugar beet increased to 200 acres between 1920 and 1980, while the production of sheep declined from 520 in 1905, to 200 by 1925, and ceased altogether by the 1930's. But, the acreage of permanent pasture increased to around 500 acres in the early 20th century to accommodate mostly up to 500 cattle. In the 1940's, there were 14 small dairy farms with 40 or more cows each – the Halls farm in Fen Road was one of these; the market was mostly local. From the 1950's, there was a decline in dairy farming with the last large herd of Friesian cattle being sold by the Easy family around 1980 to make way for the A10 bypass.

The market gardening established at the Vinery and later Alexandra Nurseries in the 19th century off the Cambridge Road, closed in 1961. The Milton Nurseries to the south of the village lasted from 1900 to 1978. Because of the large number of smallholders in the village in the early 20th century, The Milton and District Co-operative Society was formed in 1912, but with the steady decline in farming as the century progressed, the Society closed in 1962.

A legacy of Milton having once been a significant farming

village, was the founding of the Francis Jeeps Institute during the late 1960's to the 1970's by Cambridgeshire County Council on land once occupied by Manor farm between the Landbeach Road and Waterbeach Road. The school was primarily concerned with instruction in rearing livestock. Today the school has expanded to become the College of West Anglia, Cambridge, additionally supported by private funding to embrace small animal and equine husbandry courses with arable farming. Some courses are carried out in partnership with Anglia Ruskin University in Cambridge."

Dr Crowfoot rounded off this part of his tutorial by summarizing the development of Milton in the first half of the 20th century, the key features being the steady increase in population and a gradual decline in farming and the horticultural products of nurseries.

Old water goes - new water, sand, gravel and houses arrive

Dr Crowfoot then arose from his chair and went over to the small table near the window. The maps retrieved from the cupboard under the stairs at the beginning of the previous week's tutorial, were still lying on the table, held together by a piece of faded green string. "Today Tom," Dr Crowfoot exclaimed, " we are going to look at the Ordnance Survey maps dating from the beginning of the 20th century through to the present day. As before Tom, please give me a hand in spreading each map out in turn, flat on the table so that we can see how the landscape has changed in Milton between 1903 and the 1950's after the Second World War.

The first map is the O.S. Cambridgeshire Sheet XL7, (1903) – scale of 25" to 1 Mile, and the second map is the O.S. Cambridgeshire Sheet XLK7, (1927) – scale of 25" to 1 Mile. Essentially the appearance of the village in the first 30 years of the 20th century, is unchanging through the period including the First World War, except that by 1927, the War Memorial is in place at the junction of Fen Road with the High Street near the village pump and blacksmiths. However, by 1950 with reference to the

O.S. Map, Cambridgeshire Sheet TL46 – scale 1:25000, a small but central feature in the village has disappeared, the village pond (now Pond Green with the village sign); this feature once providing drinking water for farm livestock, became full of rubbish and was filled in, by the early 1930's. Another notable feature involving water which appears on this map, is the presence of the extensive gravel pits east of the Cambridge Road on land to the north of the sewage works (part of Cambridge city), and what was part of the Baitsbite enclosure fields belonging to Kings College, the earlier lands of the manor, and private freehold land."

At this point in his tutorial, Tom became aware that the appearance of the large gravel pits not far from the centre of Milton, was a dramatic change in the landscape replacing areas of previous farm land. Was this the beginning of a new era for Milton – the change in land use and therefore occupations for people in the village; indeed, had industrialisation now reached Milton? Tom posed this question to Dr Crowfoot as they both returned to their chairs by a glowing fire. Dr Crowfoot replied, "Yes Tom, between the First and Second World Wars, around 1930, after the earlier Victorian and Edwardian building phases, there was a demand for further housing developments beyond Cambridge city centre, which gave rise to the extensive building of houses to form a new suburbia. This development was typified by 1930's semi-detached houses, often with front bay windows – this building boom required much sand and gravel for mortar and driveways. Farmers and landowners with diminishing livestock, brought in companies to extract the sand and gravel from their land, (which Tom, you will recall from our first tutorial, Milton had the right geology for the minerals).

The Halls at Fen End were one of these, after Ephraim Halls had bought the freehold as a tenant farmer in 1930, from two spinsters Mary and Edith of the large farming family the Gunnells, who had a main residence at Willow farm (adjacent to the village pond on land now at the entrance to Willow Crescent). Mary and Edith

Gunnell in turn as copyholders of the manor, had purchased the freehold for the Halls farm, shortly before they sold it to Ephraim, through negotiations with the last, and non resident lady of the manor, Mary Baumgartner daughter of John Percy Baumgartner. John Baumgartner was the last resident lord of the manor at Milton Hall in the middle of the 19th century, as I mentioned in my last tutorial.

Although there had been sand and gravel extraction for centuries in the Milton area, this was from small pits providing sufficient material for the limited house building and making up of road surfaces, some of these pits are referred to in the 1802 Enclosure Award map for Milton. But, the gravel workings that arose in the 20th century at Milton, were on a large scale and occupied 30 years of activity from 1930 to the early 1960's. Within this time period, there were two further peak requirements for sand and gravel after the house building of the 1930's. The next phase of requirement for sand and gravel, was the construction of many air bases in East Anglia for the RAF in the Second World War, our nearest air base was at Waterbeach. The last phase of the requirement for sand and gravel, was the post-war building boom of houses, again extending suburbia which included Milton.

We had the building of predominantly semi-detached council houses (their pump still visible within hedges) along the Cambridge Road from the mid-1920's, then again after the Second World War, a further development of council houses was erected at Bene't Close. Prior to this in 1936, the Cambridge Concrete Company was established making roof tiles from the gault clay beneath the sand and gravel; this company was sited near some of the gravel workings at the southeast end of the village.

However, by the early 1960's, the gravel workings on most of the available land had been exhausted, and the gravel companies notably Jack Green's and M Dickerson's closed down. The majority of the gravel pit area over the next 30 years, was allowed to come under the influence of nature and become a naturalized water, rough pasture and woodland habitat setting the scene for the later Country Park. A smaller area of gravel pits at the southern end, was filled in and became part of the new industrial estate area developing to the east of the Cambridge Road."

Dr Crowfoot continued, "with reference to industrial archaeology, you will recall Tom that in our tutorial on the Romans at Milton, they established pottery kilns in the area of the gravel pits and later Country Park. A legacy of the gravel industry in the 20th century which provided artefacts of industrial archaeology, were the part buried, small gauge rail tracks and components of trucks used to convey gravel on site; these artefacts were visible for several years before the land was cleaned up for establishing the Country Park in the 1980's, we will deal with this aspect at the end of this tutorial." Dr Crowfoot concluded this part of his tutorial by saying, "that at the time the sand and gravel extraction industry ceased in the 1960's in Milton, the glasshouse industry providing salad crops and cut flowers, as mentioned earlier, also ceased. Another trade that started in the 1930's, was the laundry to the west of the High Street, this closed in the late 20th century."

New industries arrive

Tom still alert and fascinated by hearing about the volatile years of declining farming near the centre of Milton, and the rise and fall of that other land based industry, sand and gravel extraction, was now intrigued to learn more about the expansion or other industries in the village. Therefore without hesitation, Tom put a question to Dr Crowfoot. "You have just mentioned that the industrial estate developed at the southeastern end of Milton and that gravel pits were filled in nearby. I am curious to know when this industrial estate started developing, and how much of the reconstituted land from the filled in gravel pits became part of the industrial estate?" Dr Crowfoot said to Tom, "you have presented me with the right question – I was at the point of providing you with this information, a logical follow on to take us into the development of industry in Milton in the second half of the 20th century to the present day."

Dr Crowfoot continued. "The first phase of the development of the industrial estate started around 1955 on land south of the present recreation ground off Coles Road, and to the west of the large existing gravel pit in the Country Park adjacent to the visitor's centre; we will deal with the Country Park at the end of this tutorial. The first work units were involved in a diversity of products ranging from Christmas decorations, upholstery to electronics etc. By 1985, there were 15 firms involved with the building trade, engineering and scientific instruments. Many of these units came into existence as part of the second phase of the industrial estate on the reclaimed land, once gravel pits, now adjacent to the A14 trunk road. The extension of the industrial area led to the Cambridge News works being moved here, together with other printing, copying and computer firms in the late 20th century. However, although all this industry was being established in the village, by 1980 more than half the village's working population worked outside the parish of Milton, commuting mainly to Cambridge or other village work places; this left only 7% actually working in the village."

Dr Crowfoot then rounded off his reference to the industrial estate in Milton village, by saying, " we must not forget Tom, that there is Milton village and Milton parish. At the southeastern extremity of the parish bordering Chesterton to the east of the junction of the Ely railway line with the old St Ives railway line, and close to the River Cam, is another Fen Road starting in Chesterton and running north over the level crossing. This narrow road terminates just before the raised A14. On the right between the road and the river is another small modern industrial complex of work units to the south, while to the north is a residential area of modest housing units.

Milton was now a 'dormitory' village, an extended suburban annex to the city of Cambridge. Over a 100 years, Milton had evolved from the authority of the manor and church, to local authority control under the Chesterton Rural District Council at the end of the 19th century, together with the inception of its parish council. In 1974, the Chesterton Rural District Council transferred its authority to the South Cambridgeshire District Council."

The era of major house building

Tom was aware that there was this concentrated industrial area to the right as you entered Milton from Cambridge, but he knew few people who worked there and lived in the village. Tom's parents were always referring to people they knew in Milton, but they worked elsewhere. But now, Milton was a large residential village, when did the housing develop to accommodate the current population of over 4000? Dr Crowfoot looked at Tom as though he was expecting him to raise the question of continued housing development after the Second World War to house the present population of Milton, therefore Dr Crowfoot went straight into the next topic in his tutorial.

"We have the expanded industrial area in Milton, so let us take a look at the parallel increase in housing in the village in the last 50 years. After the development of Bene't Close, from the late 1950's there was a continuous period of house building on land surrounding the main old roads of Milton. We start with the development of Coles Road, Wilson Way and Old School Lane with Pryor Close, on land south of Fen Road and lying between the High Street, Cambridge Road and the remaining gravel pits. Some of this land arose from the sale of land at Halls farm at Fen End off Fen Road when it ceased to be a farm in the early 1960's, and also adjacent land of King's College associated with Coles House. You will note the naming of the roads after past residents of Milton, or places in the village, a tradition carried through to the present day.

After this, a large area of development followed. In the 1960's onwards, Goding Way (a misnomer for Goodin – an old local farming family) where Goodin's farm used to be to the north of Fen Road, then later Shirley (past landowner) and Pearson's Closes (past farmer at Fen Farm) to the south of Fen Road, and further towards the river on the right hand side of Fen Road, a mixture of houses and bungalows opposite Hill Close. After the demolition of the primary school in Fen Road in the late 1960's, a close called Hall End led off Fen Road at this point. Housing developments on the west side of Milton also got under way from the 1960's. These included Cherry Close, Willow Crescent (once associated with the Gunnells, the old village farming family who resided at Willow Farm), and Knights (lords of the manor) Way on land adjacent to the West Lodge of Milton Hall. Cul-de-sacs developed off Butt Lane from the 1960's. These were first Lyndhurst Close near the primary school which opened in 1959, replacing the old primary school in Fen Road. Then followed Fox's Close referred to earlier and later Ken's Way (after the local historian, parish and district councillor Ken Humphries whose house was on this site). Two later closes developed after local names to the south of Butt Lane, these were Coulson Close and Peter Goodin Close. Two other small cul-de-sacs developed in the village at the end of this period of building, they were Walkling Way and Recreation Close off Coles Road.

But, the largest housing development to occur in Milton was Milton Park starting in the 1980's on land previously occupied by nurseries and cattle to the west of the Cambridge Road; this is where your parents' house is Tom. This extensive development of mixed housing occurred around two main 'crescent' roads i.e. The Rowans and The Sycamores – small closes were spurs off these main roads. The final stage of this major development occurred north of Butt Lane with spine roads Humphries Way (a second recognition of Ken Humphries), and Fromont Way, again small cul-de-sacs with old Milton family names, developed off these two main roads. Road access to this development is through Humphries Way connecting with the Landbeach Road. Very recently, a new housing development has become established on land, previously the EDF site behind Milton Hall. This development has allowed for football pitches and a sports pavilion at the eastern end of the field adjacent to Long Meadow, the site of our Romano-British settlement discussed in an earlier tutorial on the Romans. The Humphrey Repton lake and surrounding woodland has been embraced into the housing development, and has accordingly been restored with considerations for wild life conservation; the development is called North Lodge Park after the listed and restored North Lodge near the entrance to the development. Now Tom, it is at this point that we must look at a major development in the infrastructure of roads linking Milton to Cambridge, and eventually other towns and cities in the UK."

New major roads

Dr Crowfoot then embarked on a brief description of three major road developments effecting Milton. "We have mentioned earlier Tom," Dr Crowfoot continued, "that a major factor which caused Milton to develop in the post Second World War years, was reasonably priced houses for people to move out of Cambridge to this new suburbia, Milton, as well as from other areas. As we have realized, most of the increase in population in Milton did not work in the village, but commuted to work elsewhere. This led to the existing A10, and through roads such as the old A45, and A604 (on the course of the Roman Road the Via Devana from Colchester to Godmanchester through Cambridge), becoming congested in the city. Therefore, in the 1970's, an A10 bypass was constructed to the west of the Milton Park development which connected with the a new A45, later A14 northern bypass, dual carriage way around the north of Cambridge; this connection was the large roundabout we have today south of Milton. The new A14 severed the old A10 road from the village into Cambridge, so that the old A10 road through Milton was de-trunked. At the end of the 20th century the 'Jane Coston' pedestrian and cycle bridge over the A14 was constructed on the course of the old A10 (Jane Coston is a past parish and county councillor living in the village). The northern end of the A10 bypass connected with Humphries Way near the Landbeach Road, before merging with the old A10 (the old Ely Road from Milton), north of the village allotments. The old Ely Road was connected to the High Street in Milton during the early 1960's by a road which cut through Milton Hall grounds from the position of North Lodge, to the junction of the High Street with Fen Road. This was the reason for moving the War Memorial mentioned earlier, to its new site in Coles Road.

Three miles west of the A14/A10 interchange at Milton, the northern bypass joined with that other new road, the M11 at Girton. All these new roads were opened in 1978 and enabled Milton to be connected to the national network of major roads. So Tom, you could more easily travel anywhere from Milton, though the general limiting factor of smooth travel, is still congestion on any of our roads in Britain; in this regard, improvements are planned for the A14 around Cambridge. One development in Milton parish which has benefited from the new road infrastructure, is the development of the Cambridge Science Park – this is my penultimate topic for today's tutorial."

The Cambridge Science Park

"The Cambridge Science Park Tom," Dr Crowfoot spoke with an emphatic tone, "was one of the most innovative schemes to arise in the 20th century for the cause of taking advances in basic academic research to commercial applications. With Cambridge University being a world leading university in science, a tradition going back several centuries to people like Sir Isaac Newton mathematician famed for demonstrating the law of gravity with an apple falling from a tree, and forward in time to Francis Crick and James Watson for discovering the structure of DNA, it is perhaps not surprising that a science park should arise close to the prestigious university – and it was to be in our parish of Milton! The idea for a science park in Cambridge, was first muted in 1969 and was pioneered by Dr John Bradfield, Senior Bursar at Trinity College, Cambridge; the land for the prospective science park was owned by Trinity College. But, Tom, before we consider briefly a few more facts about the science park, we will take a look at the archaeology that has come to light on the Trinity College land where the park has developed."

"You will recall Tom", said Dr Crowfoot, "that in our tutorial on the 'First Inhabitants', some Neolithic and Bronze Age flints were found on the Trinity College land west of the old A10 between Milton and Cambridge, and now the Science Park. But, more recently, the Cambridge Archaeological Unit reported in 2007 on excavations carried out on a 2-5 hectares area of the Science Park land adjacent to the slip road from the roundabout going west on to the A14. From 11 trenches excavated, arose Late Bronze Age and Early Iron Age pottery sherds, in keeping with that found earlier at the Landfill Site north of the A14 and south of Butt Lane. However, coming forward over 2 millenia into the 21st century, the recent excavations at the Science Park, exposed some distinctive industrial archaeology. Fragments of brick, concrete and armoured vehicle components, were found placed on top of the top soil so that any underlying earlier archaeology would not be disturbed. The armoured vehicle components consisted of sprung seats, turrets with antenna outlets, wheels, wheel-tracks and 'body parts' from track landing vehicles, either American Mark-4, or British Water Buffalo amphibious vehicles. These vehicles were made for use in the Second World War, notably for the D-Day landings in June 1944; the vehicles could have been easily transported from the railway sidings at the Science Park site, to the national railway network including the south coast of England. Aerial photographs of Milton during the 1940's, show a complex of workshops and tank storage buildings at the centre position of the present Science Park site, and north of numerous railway sidings which connected to the Cambridge to St Ives railway line.

This war time site was abandoned after 1950 and the structures demolished. Before and continuing after the Second World War, some of the land at the Science Park site was rough pasture farmland for Trinity Farm keeping livestock such as cattle and pigs. We can see the location of this farm Tom, on the O.S. reprinted map of 1961. There is just one other feature of interest in our parish related to the 2nd World War, and that is the presence of two concrete 'pill boxes' near the tow path by the River Cam before the parish boundary with Waterbeach. These structures were built for defence purposes to house guns and light ammunition in the event that the Germans landed in Britain and entered the country from the Wash and the Ouse catchment area; fortunately for us this never happened."

Tom was fascinated by the presence of artefacts related to industrial archaeology being found in Milton, and linked to one of the major traumatic events his country became involved in during the 20th century – a time just before his parents were born, and certainly, his grandparents could vividly remember. And then, what a change of industrial product, from war to peace, heavy industry to high-technical output; Tom's village Milton has certainly witnessed, a very recent rapid evolution of industry from farming to the latest science based light industry. This awareness, Tom had to reveal to Dr Crowfoot who was pleased that his tutorial was having such an impact. But, Dr Crowfoot had more to say about the development of the Cambridge Science Park in the last 40 years since the first buildings were erected.

"In my closing words on the Science Park Tom, I want to provide you with a perspective of the area of land involved and the change in landscape as the work units and buildings were erected. The Cambridge Science Park was developed on 126 acres of land which had been acquired by Trinity College over 500 years, as follows: 70 acres in 1443, 49 acres in 1846, and 7 acres in 1978 – all on 2nd terrace alluvial gravels. During the Second World War, about half the land was requisitioned for the armoured vehicles and railway sidings. Although later, the site became classified as a Green Belt site with potential restrictions on development, an application to develop the site for the Science Park was approved on the condition that there was a sensitivity for the nature of the landscape, and so development got under way."

Dr Crowfoot continued, "the first building was occupied in 1973 by Laser-Scan, dealing with computer controlled applications. By 1984, there were 25 tenants occupied in a wide range of technologies employing 764 people. Until the present day, the Science Park has continued to expand over several phases of building and Milton parish council is continually receiving applications through the South Cambridgeshire District Council, to pass comment on the plans. The A14 and A10 with the adjacent dual carriage way into Cambridge passing the main entrance into the Science Park, and since 2011, the Guided Bus on the track line of the old St Ives railway line, enables the large number of people working at the Science Park and in other buildings nearby on Cambridge city land, to arrive at their work places.

One of the first distinctive buildings to appear at the Science Park, was NAPP pharmaceutical, an imposing white concrete and glass building, very futuristic in appearance, best seen from the A14/A10 roundabout on leaving Milton. This building rightly or wrongly, has been likened to a 'concrete toast rack'. The NAPP building and others, harbouring the technological applications of the latest advances in science, appropriately constitute the context of 'The Cambridge Phenomenon' or 'Silicon Fen' after a similar high-tec area in America called 'Silicon Valley'. Some of the technical, maintenance and office staff who work at the Science Park and elsewhere, may have received further education training at the Cambridge Regional College (CRC) which is situated to the west of the Science park in the extreme southwest corner of Milton Parish between the Mere Way and the guided Bus track. Traces of earthworks existed here known as 'King's Hedges' and several Roman coins have been found on this site."

'New lamps for old'

"The establishment of science parks, is a modern phenomenon, but in addition to these sites, is the conversion of large old houses, often with land to accommodate offices, laboratories and workshops directed towards technical industries. Here again Tom," said Dr Crowfoot, "Milton is at the forefront. Our last manor house Milton Hall, after the Second World War, was taken over by Eastern Electricity. You could pay your electricity bill at the offices established in the rooms of the Hall, while workshops were built to the rear for the maintenance of vehicles and training of apprentices for electrical installations. The field behind the Hall was also used for this training – erecting posts for supporting overhead electricity cables.

The Hall itself was extended for further facilities, but this time with the exodus of Eastern Electricity, the Hall with its new extensions, was occupied by high-tec organisations. Clive Sinclair the Cambridge entrepreneur, was one of the first occupants – the inventor of the classic early computer for home use, the ZX Spectrum. This was followed by his abortive C5 electrically powered, 'buggy' styled tricycle. In the last 30 years after Sinclair, there has been a number of high-tec firms occupying the Hall. EDF electricity company, used the workshops and training field vacated by Eastern Electricity. It is the workshop area and training field that has been purchased by Bellway Homes for the development of North Lodge Park housing, and football pitches set within the Humphrey Repton landscape which includes the restored lake. The Hall itself has been restored for offices."

New amenities for a 'new' village

"The final part of our last tutorial Tom, is to look at the amenities that have accompanied the modern development of Milton with its increased population and work places." Dr Crowfoot put a question to Tom. "What amenities in Milton have made you and your parents consider that Milton is a good place to live?" This question made Tom think hard, but it was not long after a brief pause, that he began to list a number of those aspects about living in Milton which he considered a great advantage in the modern world. "The obvious advantages," Tom enthusiastically revealed, "are the proximity to Cambridge with relative ease of travel either by car, bus or bicycle into the city. This is achieved by good roads and cycle tracks, the latter either the direct route into Cambridge over the Jane Coston Bridge, or a delightful route as I know being a cyclist, is along the tow path by the River from the end of Fen Road into Cambridge. But back in the village, we have a Tesco supermarket, a veterinary practice, three recreation grounds, the largest at the centre of the village with a Community Centre and nearby doctors' surgery. An extension of the sports facilities, is the golf course opposite the allotments which in themselves are an amenity for growing your food with healthy exercise a bonus. Furthermore, we are privileged to have the Country Park on our doorstep with its protective wooded walks, lakes for observing wild fowl and fishing, open areas for picnics and games, and a visitor centre for refreshments and social events." Dr Crowfoot replied, "a very comprehensive list Tom, but I would like to expand a little more with reference to the history of these amenities. I will deal with them in the order you dealt with them. When you cycle or walk on the tow path along the River in the direction of Cambridge, you soon arrive at Baitsbite Lock with its grey brick, 19th century lock keeper's cottage (now occupied by Cam Conservancy staff). The lock controls river levels and allows for river craft to move through the lock. Only a few decades ago, the lock was controlled manually by a lock keeper as had been the case for well over a 100 years, but now the water levels are automatically controlled, and passage of river craft is enabled by electrically controlled lock gates which are the old hand - push and pull gates, once operated by the lock keeper with a pole. This pole was also used to move a small bridge across the lock for pedestrians and cyclists to continue to Horningsea or Fen Ditton; this has been replaced by a fixed bridge raised over the lock. The tow path was used by horses to tow the barges along the river before these were phased out with the increase in road and rail freight.

Returning to the village, the Tesco store was built at the time the Milton Park housing development occurred and opened in the late 1980's. Tesco also provided the land for the second recreation ground behind the store towards the A14/A10 roundabout, together with a substantial grant for a sports pavilion. The Community Centre at the end of Cole's Road, replaced a simple wood and glazed village hall, and was opened by Francis Pym MP in 1986. Land adjacent to the Centre by the Country Park, was another gravel pit called Middleton Pit; this was filled in to provide football pitches over 30 years ago. Briefly, the other amenities we have in Milton are a good primary school and two churches."

"But finally, this leaves two areas of land which provide extremely useful amenities for Milton and elsewhere." said Dr Crowfoot in summing up. "You have referred to both of these Tom, but now a few more details. With regard to bus travel, we have reviewed the land off Butt Lane for its archaeology in a previous tutorial. Part of this land nearest the village became the new Park and Ride site in 2009 for the bus service to Cambridge, and beyond to the Babraham Road including the nationwide renowned Addenbrookes Hospital. Access to the Park and Ride site is obviously by road including the A10 bypass. For access by foot or bicycle, there is a a bridge over the bypass, initially built to enable people to continue their journey along Butt Lane towards Impington including access to the Roman road, the Mere Way. When you stand on the bridge and look south towards Cambridge, significant buildings in the city such as church spires, are no longer visible from here due to the filling in of the first landfill site between the A14 and A10 interchange. The filled in site was capped with a large amount of soil and sown with grass giving rise to an artificial hill known as the 'Milton Mountain', dramatically changing the landscape.

Milton Country Park

Now to our second area of land, over 90 acres, to conclude this tutorial, it is Milton Country Park." Once again, Dr Crowfoot had the various maps at the ready, that he and Tom had already referred to. " Earlier in the tutorial Tom, I mentioned that after the gravel pits ceased to provide further sand and gravel in the 1960's, they were left to become naturalized. In this regard, if you have the opportunity to see one of the many large white willows present in the Park, cut down by a saw, count the number of growth rings across the trunk. You will often be able to count up to 50 rings indicating that the tree was 50 years old, the beginning of the naturalization of the gravel pit area by a distinctive fenland tree. Another species of tree of possible historical interest, is the aspen seen as rampant copses between Todd's and Dickerson's pits at the north, and south end corner by the 13th public drain, and at the southeast corner of Dickerson's pit near the footbridge over the drain. This tree may have been planted for firewood or making furniture. The land belonged to a number of owners, one being Cambridgeshire County Council after Dennis Halls, son of the now deceased Ephraim, who had sold land for the housing development in Old School Lane, sold the remainder to another person, who in turn sold most of the land to the County Council. This land at the centre of the present Country Park with Hall's pool, the adjacent large gravel pits - Todd's and Dickerson's, land to the south of this area east of the industrial estate, and the parish's nature reserve Tomkins Mead, all came under the authority of the County Council. This large area of land was minimally landscaped with access paths for the natural environs of the area, with bridges constructed over the 13th public drain, a visitor centre built facing Todd's Pit at its southern end, and a nearby children's play area installed; a large grass picnic area which included the D-Day Remembrance Meadow, and a car park with a toilet block completed the establishment of Milton Country Park. Features worth noting on the footpath around the northeast corner of Dickerson's pit, are the concrete bases for three chalets put in place before the establishment of the Country Park. However, planning permission was refused and the chalets were never built. The Park was opened in May 1993 and administered by the South Cambridgeshire District Council. At the end of the first decade of the 21st century, the South Cambridgeshire District Council handed over the management of the Park in May 2008, to a private organisation, Cambridge Sport Lakes Trust. This trust may expand the recreational amenities of the area, by constructing the extensive and long proposed rowing lake between Milton and Waterbeach; this will be an opportunity for further archaeology.

The Park is visited by people, not only from Milton but from Cambridge city and further away to partake in, not only the activities provided by a natural outdoor environment, such as walking, jogging, fishing, bird watching and photography, but also organised events such as charity fun runs, various shows and festivals, and children's activities. While dipping in Hall's Pool for sticklebacks, the children may be lucky to see a medium size brown 'dog' dashing across the path, but it is not a dog, it is a Muntjac deer behaving like the many species of dragonflies and damselflies – darting around the open spaces in the Park, you have probably seen all this wildlife Tom." "Yes I have, particularly in August," replied Tom.

"In conclusion Tom, with regard to life in Milton and all its amenities, during the Millenium year 2000, photographs of daily activities and places in the village, were taken every day of the year. This resulted in the photographs being published in a book, "Milton 2000: a Daily Photographic Record" which was made available to those living in Milton – such an excellent way of recording life in our village at this milestone in time after a journey that started before 2000 years ago."

In war, plans for peace

Dr Crowfoot momentarily closed his eyes before looking straight at Tom with a relaxed smile, "and that is the end of the last tutorial! But one final comment, in the Second World War, there was a group of academics in the Department of Town Planning, University College, London whose minds were beyond the War; they were considering improvement plans for extending amenities associated with extra housing in towns and villages around Britain after the War; one of the villages was Milton. A number of maps of Milton were produced showing vast changes to the landscape of the village with new houses, shops, schools and churches, cinemas, swimming pools and other sports facilities etc., virtually another new town. In four maps the largest old buildings of significance were retained i.e. All Saints' Church, the rectory, Milton Hall and Coles House (except on one map); some other old buildings like public houses were also retained. But the features on the maps which did arise 30 years later, were the A10 bypass (some showing a dual carriage way), and extensive housing between the bypass and the High Street. Although there was housing planned to the east of the High Street, this was greater than has happened in the Coles Road area in some plans, and as yet extensive building of houses north of Fen Road shown on some of the maps, has not occurred, apart from the new North Lodge Park development – fortunately the rural landscape around the Humphry Repton lake was retained as now."

Goodbye to Kiln Cottage

Dr Crowfoot and Tom arose from their respective chairs, collected the rolled maps together and left the warmth of the log fire with the grandfather clock in the hall striking 10 o'clock for the last time at the end of a these tutorials on a Saturday morning. As they put the maps back in the cupboard under the stairs, Tom felt a soft nudge against his ankles – it was Caesar, sensing like all cats that this human guest was leaving, perhaps for the last time. Tom bent down and stroked Caesar's back, the cat replied with a friendly purr while accompanying his master and Tom to the front door. " Have you got room for this Tom in your saddle bag," a cheery motherly voice called from the kitchen: it was Mrs Crowfoot, she was holding a spicy, fruity-smelling cake, removed from the oven sometime towards the end of Tom's tutorial and now cool enough to handle. "This is for you and your parents to have with a cup of tea over this cold weekend," said Mrs Crowfoot. "Oh, thank you so much," said Tom, "I am most grateful, what a kind thought, and thank you, to you too Dr Crowfoot, for such a comprehensive and stimulating series of tutorials. The information you have given me about the archaeology of Milton in an historical context will be a great help to me in choosing my 'A' level project." "It has been a great pleasure to provide you with these extra lessons Tom," said Dr Crowfoot as he opened the front door. "I have given you far more information than you will need for your 'A' level, but then you knew that, because of your general interest in the local history of Milton, this was an opportunity to receive the extra information."

As Tom carefully placed Mrs Crowfoot's cake in his saddle bag, with Dr and Mrs Crowfoot, and Caesar waiting to say "Goodbye" at the door step, Dr Crowfoot said a few more words to Tom. "Tom, your parents have invited me to your house over afternoon tea to discuss what opportunities there might be for you when you leave the 6th form college, with hopefully your desired 'A' levels passed with a good mark next summer. They suggest tomorrow afternoon, if not too soon. Perhaps, not being too impertinent, I can enjoy a piece of my wife's cake with you, she knows how much I like her cooking. See you tomorrow then Tom, and thanks for being such an attentive student." With that, Tom set off along Fen Road on his bicycle towards home, turning round to wave to his tutor, his wife and their wise old feline – they returned a wave from two hands, and for a moment Tom also thought, from a paw too.

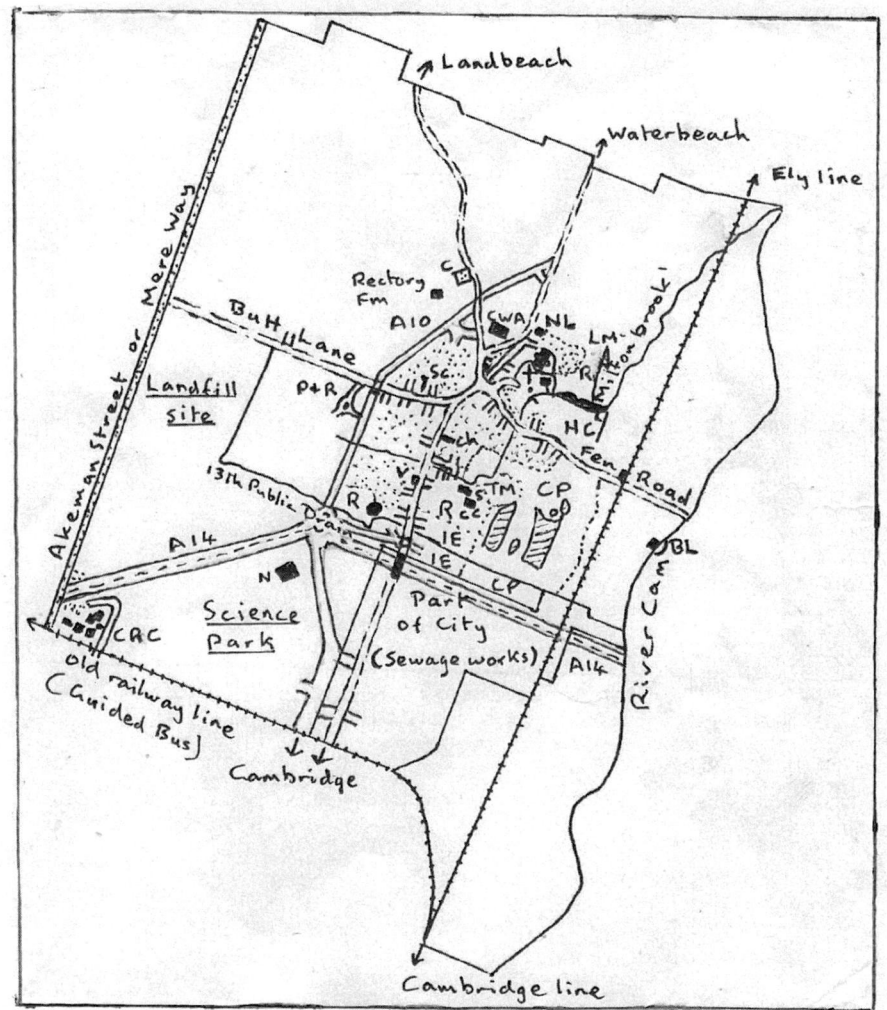

92. Sketch map of the development of Milton village by 2014.

CWA College of West Anglia; **Sc** Primary School; **R** recreation ground; **c** cemetery;
LM Long Meadow; **HC** Hill close; **P & R** Park & Ride; **V** veterinary practice;
S doctors' surgery; **cc** community centre; **CP** Country Park; **TM** Tomkin's Mead;
IE industrial estate; **N** NAPP building; **CRC** Cambridge Regional College;
BL Baitsbite lock;   housing area;   new roads leading off old roads;
ch chapel; † All Saints' Church;   Milton Hall; **NL** North Lodge;
• remaining fish pond in 'Each' garden;   ● Tesco superstore

93. Ephraim Halls with his family outside their house in Fen Road c.1930-'31 after they had bought the freehold from the Gunnell family, who in turn had bought the freehold from the last lady of the manor, Mary Baumgartner (not in residence) when the Gunnells were the copyholders.

(Dennis Halls, with permission)

94. Dennis Halls (the only son and last to farm the Halls farm), seated on on his Fordson tractor at the rear of the farm in the 1950's.

(Dennis Halls, with permission)

95. Aerial view of Halls Farm (centre), 18th century mansard roof cottage (left), Cole's House (right) and Goding Way a new housing development off Fen Road (bottom), c. 1960.

(Dennis Halls, with permission)

96. Fields with cereal crop and residential caravans on previously Halls Farm land (now part of Milton Country Park) c. 1962-'64. Note new houses in Old School Lane behind caravans.

(Dennis Halls, with permission)

97. The NAPP buildings, one of the original and more grand developments at the Science Park. Note the A1309 dual carriage way which replaced the A10 on the Cambridge side of the A14 to provide the main access to the Science Park.

98. The 'Jane Coston' bridge over the A14, built to provide a more direct route between Milton and Cambridge by bicycle or on foot. In the photograph, Milton is to the left, and Cambridge to the right.

99. Another view of the 'Jane Coston' bridge as seen from Cowley Road on the Cambridge side of the A14.

100. The cycle/footbridge over the A10 bypass in 2007, showing the initial trenches for archaeology on the site of the later Park and Ride at Milton.

101. Baitsbite lock looking north with the gates being repaired. Note revolving footbridge across the lock which was manoeuvred to the lock path (foreground) by the lock keeper using a long pole which also moved the gates. The footbridge was replaced later by a metal 'up and over' bridge, over 20 years ago, and the gates became electrically operated.

102. One of the two World War 2 'pill boxes' adjacent to the tow path along the River Cam towards the parish boundary with Waterbeach. These structures were built for defence purposes to house light ammunition and guns, in the event that the Germans entered the country via the Wash and its associated rivers.

103. Hall's Pool, view looking east through hawthorn copse adjacent to Dickerson's old gravel pit in Milton Country Park.

104. Winter scene at the D-Day Remembrance Meadow in Milton Country Park. Note the monolith with remembrance details in the distance above the bench. The associated trees of English oak, American oak and Canadian maple represent the three main countries whose military forces were engaged in the D-Day landing on the Normandy beaches, 6 June 1944.

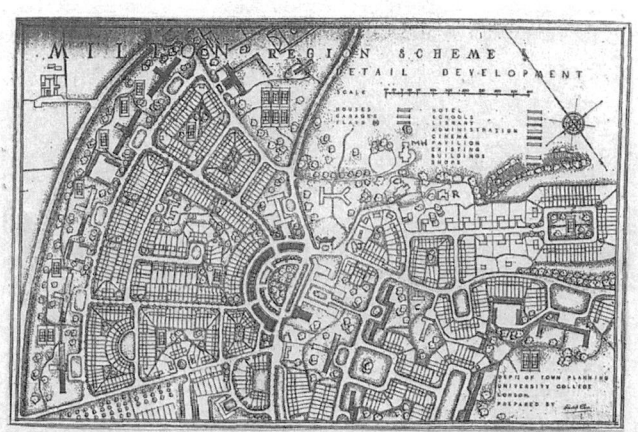

105. In the 1940's, minds of academics at the Department of Town Planning, University College, London, were beyond the War. Plans were considered for improving the amenities of many towns and villages, Milton was one of these. Of 4 plans, the one here shows considerable development at the centre of the village. Note, some of this has happened, including the A10 bypass. Some older properties have been retained: ch, the church; MH, Milton Hall; R, rectory; c, Cole's House; J, the Jolly Brewers public house.
(Cambridgeshire Collection, with permission)

106. We end where we started. When Sir Cyril Fox produced his epic book, 'The Archaeology of the Cambridge Region' in 1923, he was living at the Red Gables next to The White Horse' public house on the High Street, Milton. Since that time, much archaeology has been carried out, and historic and landscape changes have occurred in the village as revealed in 'Milton through Time'.
(Cambridgeshire Collection, with permission)

8. Where from here?

A little more than 24 hours had gone by after Tom's last tutorial with Dr Crowfoot, when Dr Crowfoot rang the front door bell at Tom's parents' house; this was situated among other new houses built at Milton Park to the west of the High Street in the 1980's. It was 3.00 pm, the time arranged for Dr Crowfoot to visit Tom's parents, and together with Tom, discuss Tom's future prospects after he had hopefully achieved his 'A' level results in just under two years time.

Tom's father opened the door to greet Dr Crowfoot, "Good afternoon Charles, it is a pleasure to meet you again, you seem to have been putting Tom through his paces on the archaeology and aspects of local history of Milton, come through to the lounge," said Tom's father after a warm handshake with Dr Crowfoot.

In the lounge was seated Tom's mother next to Tom on a settee, while Tom's father said to Dr Crowfoot, "please sit in this armchair on the other side of the fireplace." But there was no real fire in this modern house, only an electric fire made to look like a real coal fire to back up the gas fired central heating, particularly when the central heating was turned off on warmer days. The décor, curtains, carpets and furniture were all contemporary here by contrast with that in Dr Crowfoot's house, Kiln Cottage – a time warp to earlier times and fashion. In the centre of the room was a glass and metal coffee table with enough plates, cups and saucers, cutlery, milk and sugar for four people, but something was missing – the teapot and some sort of cake or scones. But Tom's mother needed no prompting, she was off to the kitchen to complete the items on the table. After a few minutes while Tom, his father (who was now sitting in the remaining armchair), and Dr Crowfoot were having a casual conversation about coming events in the village, Tom's mother returned with a tray on which was the teapot, some scones, butter and jam, and, the fruit cake that Mrs

Crowfoot had given Tom yesterday.

When Dr Crowfoot saw the homely array of accessories to a cup of tea, his eyes lit up, particularly when they caught sight of his wife's cake. Tom had acted on Dr Crowfoot's hope that there might be scope for consuming a small portion of his wife's irresistible cake. But being polite, when Tom's mother offered Dr Crowfoot the goodies, he chose the equally delightful scones and jam that Tom's mother had just cooked, then with a second cup of tea, he had a slice of Mrs Crowfoot's cake which all present consumed with complementary comments – both cake and scones. With everyone relaxed by this mid-afternoon refreshment, it was time to get down to the main purpose of the get together on this late autumn Sunday afternoon, with the last rays of the setting sun just reaching the settee through the French windows.

Careers for archaeologists

Tom's father spoke first, "Charles, we invited you here this afternoon for your advice following Tom hopefully obtaining his 'A' level in archaeology together with his other chosen 'A' level subjects, what further education and career prospects would be open to him?" Dr Crowfoot sat upright and leaning back slightly, replied, "there are least three main career routes Tom could take, i.e. becoming a professional archaeologist working either in the field, or as an archivist for background knowledge to sites for excavation, then there is museum work, and lastly education, teaching at the level of secondary education or higher education. Let us deal with each of these prospective careers in turn.

With Tom's interest primarily in archaeology, I hope he will want go to a university to study for a degree in archaeology pending him passing his 'A' levels with an adequate grade for university entrance, different universities will require different combinations of grades. Obviously with archaeology being Tom's main degree subject, he will be carrying out some field work during his degree course, often carried out in the long summer vacation. At some universities e.g. Cambridge, archaeology and anthropology are studied. Options in anthropology are social anthropology and biological anthropology, the latter with an emphasis on scientific aspects involving human anatomy with laboratory support for studying bone structure and chemistry (including carbon 14 and DNA determinations); *this has been so important for identifying the recently discovered skeleton of Richard III under a car park in Leicester.*

Having obtained a bachelor's degree, Tom could either apply for a job as a field archaeologist or in archives with one of the local authorities, or increasingly, with one of the commercial organisations involved in excavations prior to housing, industrial or transport developments. Opportunities often arise for archaeologists working for local authorities or in higher education, to become involved in out-reach work, involving schools and the general public, this area is very active in Cambridge.

But, if Tom obtained a good degree, he should consider studying for a master's or PhD degree involving research. Achieving a postgraduate degree will provide Tom with a greater chance of obtaining a senior position in his employment as a professional archaeologist. Many professional archaeologists become Members of the Institute for Field Archaeologists (MIFA)."

"Now to the second option, museum work," Dr Crowfoot continued. "Entrance to this occupation is more varied than becoming a professional field archaeologist. You can become employed by a museum straight from school with GCSE's or 'A' level, and continue with part-time NVQ qualifications at a college of further education while in employment at a museum. Alternatively, with your first degree and ideally, postgraduate degree as mentioned for opportunities as a field archaeologist, this will provide more scope for a senior position in a museum i.e. becoming a curator or senior administrator. Here a master's degree in museology or business administration could be an advantage. For example, Manchester University offers an MA in museum and galleries studies, while Leicester University offers a postgraduate degree in social history and archaeology. Employees in museums are encouraged to become Members of the Museums Association."

"Our third option," Dr Crowfoot concluded, "is to become a teacher. This profession exists at many levels, in primary and secondary schools, and in further and higher education. A desirable postgraduate qualification for teaching in schools and museum work involving communication with the general public, is the Postgraduate Certificate in Education (PGCE). An archaeology graduate will often have a qualification in history, the subject taught in schools, rather than archaeology as a separate subject, Tom's school is an exception. In institutions involved with further and higher education, higher degrees are a usual qualification for posts in these institutions. Then there are diplomas in archaeology offered by several educational establishments as full or part-time courses; these qualifications are often accepted as an alternative to a first degree for employment.

Finally, there is just one other area where archaeologists are employed, often after several years' experience. This area includes organisations such as English Heritage, The National Trust, the Council for British Archaeology, various archaeological trusts, and at stately homes being in charge of existing and future archaeological aspects of the estate."

Prospects for employment

With these words, Dr Crowfoot finished his informative advice on career prospects in archaeology and commented, "do you have any questions?" Almost simultaneously, Tom and his parents replied, "what are the prospects for employment in archaeology in those areas you have defined?" Dr Crowfoot hesitated for a moment, "whatever qualifications you finally achieve Tom, they will not guarantee you employment, it is a competitive world out there, and this applies to many fields of employment. However, in your case Tom, if you maintain the positive motivation you have shown to me during the course of my tutorials and likewise, I assume in your 'A' level work, I am confident that you will find employment in archaeology associated with history, which will suit you."

As the sun had now set behind neighbouring houses, in turn, Tom and his parents gratefully thanked Dr Crowfoot for all the time he had spent tutoring Tom about the archaeology and aspects of the local history of Milton. Furthermore, Tom's parents were confident that Dr Crowfoot's efforts would be rewarded by Tom achieving a good pass in his 'A' level archaeology. Dr Crowfoot acknowledged this thanks, by replying as they all left the lounge and walked towards the front door, "thank you for your kind remarks, it has been a great pleasure to provide the tutorials to Tom and it gave me the opportunity to pull all the information about the archaeology of Milton together and to elaborate on this with related historical topics. There is still potential to discover more archaeology in Milton i.e. with excavations being carried out sometime in the future on the site of the Romano-British farmstead in Long Meadow and Hill Close, and the site of the medieval manor also at Hill Close. It would be very satisfying if someone like you Tom, having become a qualified archaeologist, could at some appropriate time in the future have the opportunity to supervise these required excavations. I am still curious to know where the Romano-British were buried, and likewise the Anglo-Saxons – there must be cemeteries somewhere waiting to be discovered? Perhaps these human remains will be revealed one day by developers, as Milton continues to expand and comes ever closer to the city of Cambridge as has happened with Chesterton, Trumpington and Cherry Hinton. Further information gathered here, could provide yet more understanding to the development of Milton through time."

"Milton is a village, which is a model for demonstrating the origins of a desirable place to live over thousands of years from the stone age to the present, and you Tom might have the opportunity one day to up-date the archaeology and history of Milton with a book. Now I must leave you to return home and feed Caesar the cat – I always do this in the evening. Goodbye to you all, I expect we shall see each other around the village from time to time, and let me know how your college work and your project are going Tom, and good luck with your exams."

Tom's parents opened the front door and said with Tom, "Goodbye" to Dr Crowfoot. Darkness was now descending with a chill in the air, as Tom and his parents watched Dr Crowfoot walk steadily down the road, his long white hair emerging from beneath his wide brimmed hat, reflecting the light from the street lamp, his mission accomplished.

The first village school for all, built in 1836 by King's College, Cambridge at Fen Lane (Road). The photograph was taken in 1908, where today is located the entrance to Hall End.

Note: left, caretaker's house; right, main school room.

(Cambridgeshire Collection with permission)

Further reading

The archaeology referred to in this book, is to be found in detailed reports in the Heritage and Environment Records (HER) office at Shire Hall, Cambridge; these reports can be consulted by prior arrangement with the HER. Furthermore, any questions about archaeology in Cambridgeshire including finds, should be addressed to the same office. Write to: Box CC 1008, Shire Hall, Cambridge CB3 0AP, telephone 01223 728564 or e-mail archaeology@cambridgeshire.gov.uk.

Some key reports for archaeology on the fen edge of Milton including manorial land, are given below.

Booth, W.D. (2009a) *A Preliminary Archaeological Survey (a): Long Meadow, Milton, Cambridgeshire with particular reference to Crop Marks, Geophysical Survey and Fieldwalking.* Report No.1, Parish Archaeological Warden, Milton.

Booth, W.D. (2009b) *A Preliminary Archaeological Survey (b): Hill Close, Milton, Cambridgeshire with particular reference to Crop Marks, Geophysical Survey and Fieldwalking.* Report No.2, Parish Archaeological Warden, Milton.

Clarke, G., Bullivant, M. & Booth, W.D. (2009) *Report of archaeology test pit excavation at Long Meadow & Hill Close, Fen Road, Milton, Cambridge.* Active 8 Archaeology, Cherry Hinton, Cambridge and Parish Archaeological Warden, Milton (W.D.Booth).

Frend, W.H.C. (1998) *Roman Kilns at Penfold Farm, Milton.* Proceedings of the Cambridge Antiquarian Society 87: 45-47.

Macaulay, S. (1999) *Car Dyke, Waterbeach, Cambridgeshire, Post Excavation Assessment and Updated Project Design.* Archaeological Field Unit, Cambridgeshire County Council, Report No. PXA 13.

Rees, G. (2008) *Iron Age, Roman and Medieval Settlement at Ely Road, Milton, Cambridgeshire.* Oxford Archaeology East, Archaeological Evaluation Report No. 1053 (Ref. MILHA 08).

Reynolds, A.T. & Leith, S. (1992) *Archaeology between Cambridge & Ely (The A10 corridor).* Archaeological Section, Cambridgeshire County Council Report No. 69.

Reynolds, A.T. (1994) *Iron Age/Romano-British Settlement at Milton: an Archaeological Rescue Project.* Archaeological Field Unit, Cambridgeshire County Council Report No. 104.

Robinson, B. & Guttmann, E.B. (1996) *An Archaeological Evaluation of the Proposed Rowing Site of the Cambridge Rowing Trust, Rowing Lake at Milton and Waterbeach, Cambridgeshire.* Archaeological Field Unit, Cambridgeshire County Council Report No.120.

Sanderson, I. (2008) *Milton Fen Road Geophysical Report.* Archaeology RheeSearch Report (HER: ECB 2707).

Walker, F.G. (1912) *Roman Pottery Kilns at Horningsea.* Proceedings of the Cambridge Antiquarian Society 17: 14-69.

The following is a list of publications either mentioned in the book, or recommended for background reading to the archaeology and history of Milton. Many of these publications are present in the Cambridge Collection or in the main library, at the Cambridgeshire Library, Lion Yard, Cambridge.

Carter, Norma & Watts, C. (1984) *The Cambridge Science Park, Planning and Development, Case Study 4*. The Royal Institute of Chartered Surveyors.

Child, M. (2004) *Discovering Church Architecture. A glossary of terms*. Shire Publications Ltd., Cromwell House, Church Street, Princes Risborough, Buckinghamshire HP77 9AA UK. [Note: Shire Publications have produced a large range of small books on historical topics and archaeological artefacts].

Clay, W.K. (1869) *A History of the Parish of Milton in the County of Cambridge*. Cambridge Antiquarian Society.

Dowdy, M., Miller, Judith, & Austin, D. (1997) *Be your own house detective*. BBC books, BBC Worldwide Publishing, BBC Worldwide Ltd., Woodlands, 80 Wood Lane, London W12 0TT.
[A very informative book for those with older properties wishing to know more about their origins, dating and structural features of the buildings].

Fox, C. (1923) *The Archaeology of the Cambridge Region*. University Press, Cambridge. [Digitally reprinted version, 2010].

Grove, R. (1976) *The Cambridgeshire Mining Coprolite Rush*. The Oleander Press, Cambridge, England.

Humphries, K. (1962) *The Story of Milton*. Cambridge Collection, Cambridge City Library.

Kirby, T. & Oosthuizen, Susan. [edits.] (2000) *An Atlas of Cambridgeshire and Huntingdonshire History*. Centre for Regional Studies, Anglia Polytechnic University (now Anglia Ruskin University), East Road, Cambridge CB1 1PT.

Lewis, Carenza, Mitchell-Fox, P. & Dyer, C. (2001) *Village, Hamlet and Field. Changing Medieval Settlements in Central England*. Windgather Press, 29 Bishop Road, Bollington, Macclesfield, Cheshire SK10 5NX, U.K.

Milton Parish Council (2000) *The Milton Millenium Book 2000: A Daily Photographic Record.* Milton Parish Council (Milton, Cambridgeshire) U.K.

Milton Regional Development Plan (1942-1943) Bartlett School of Architecture, London.

Malim, T. (2003) *The Anglo-Saxons in South Cambridgeshire.* Cambridgeshire County Council. [Note. A series of small books were produced between 1977 and 1978, published by The Oleander Press of Cambridge on four historical periods in Cambridgeshire. These books are *Prehistoric Cambridgeshire* by Alison Taylor, *Roman Cambridgeshire* by David M. Brown, *Anglo-Saxon Cambridgeshire* by Alison Taylor, and *Medieval Cambridgeshire* by H.C. Darby. The books are easy reading for general interest and exist in the Cambridgeshire Collection or some may still be available for purchase at Shire Hall.]

O'Connor, B. (2009/11) *Digging for Dinosaurs. (the Great Fenland Coprolite Rush).* The Ely Society.

Palmer, W. (1935) *William Cole of Milton.* Galloway & Porter, Ltd., Cambridge. [Reprinted edition with a forward by J. D. Pickles, Cambridge University Press, 2007].

Parker, R. (1975) *The Common Stream.* William Collins Sons & Co. Ltd., U.K.

Pevsner, N. (1954) *The Buildings of England: Cambridgeshire.* Penguin Books Ltd., Hardmondsworth, Middlesex.

Rackham, O. (1993) *The History of the Countryside.* J. M. Dent, London.

Taylor, Alison (1998) *Archaeology of Cambridgeshire Vol.2: South East Cambridgeshire and The Fen Edge*. Cambridgeshire County Council Resources Unit, 19 Gordon Avenue, March, Cambs. PE15 8AL.

Taylor, C. (1973) *The Cambridgeshire Landscape (Cambridgeshire and the Southern Fens)*. Hodder & Stoughton, London.

Tonks, R.S. (2009) *The Milton Chronicle 1777-1901 (extracts from the Cambridge Chronicle and University Journal)*. Milton Contact Ltd. 3 Hall End, Milton, Cambridge CB24 6AQ, U.K.

V. C. H. *The Victoria History of the Counties of England: Milton and other estates. A History of the County of Cambridgeshire and the Isle of Ely: Vol.9. Chesterton, Northstowe and Papworth Hundreds*. Institute of Historical Research, University of London.

Details of other sources of information of local historical and archaeological interest, can be found in 'The Conduit', an annual publication produced by the Cambridge Antiquarian Society. Examples are the Cambridge Archives & Local Studies and Jigsaw Cambridgeshire Community Archaeological Project. Membership of local history societies and archaeology groups, in particular the Cambridge Antiquarian Society and Cambridge Association for Local History, can also be found in 'The Conduit', which can be seen at the Cambridge City Library.

Some useful websites

An excellent comprehensive website has been created for Milton.

www.milton.org.uk

This website covers a wide range of information and activities concerned with the village both past and present as reflected in photographs and written material; a very complementary source of information to the contents of this book.

Further information on GCE archaeology at AS level on to A level, *courses, projects and examinations* (see Unit 04- Archaeological Investigations) in:

www.aqa.org.uk/qual/gce/pdf/AQA-w-sp-10.pdf/archaeology

Further information and membership of the Cambridge Antiquarian Society.

www.camantsoc.org

The Council for British Archaeology (CBA).

This is an independent charity whose essential aims are to promote and preserve Britain's heritage. The CBA produces the British 'Archaeology' magazine and other books and publications. The organisation is divided into regions, for Cambridgeshire it is CBA East with annual membership fees of £5 for individuals and joint membership, or £7 for institutions. The CBA advertises job vacancies and encourages volunteers to become involved in their excavations. Furthermore, the CBA becomes involved in an Annual Festival of Archaeology, which for Cambridgeshire, archaeological excavations with volunteers at Wimpole, has been a popular venue as part of the festival's activities. The festival occurs at the end of July.

Contact details: www.britarch.ac.uk , Tel. 0194 671 417
e-mail: admin@britarch.ac.uk

Continuing Education.

The Institute of Continuing Education (ICE) based at Madingley Hall, in the University of Cambridge, offers part-time courses in archaeology and local history. These courses are open to anyone with an interest in the subject, without the need for special qualifications i.e.

(i) the Undergraduate Certificate in Archaeology (1 yr)
(1st year undergraduate level)

(ii) the Undergraduate Diploma in Archaeology (1 yr)
(2nd year undergraduate level)

(iii) the Undergraduate Advanced Diploma in Archaeology
(2 yrs) (3rd year undergraduate level)

Contact details: http://www.ice.cam.ac.uk

Anglia Ruskin University offers a part time and full time BA (Hons) degree in Archaeology and Landscape History at their University Centre in Peterborough. The course deals with theory and practice, providing students with the knowledge and skills to work in archaeology, museums and archives.

Contact details:

www.anglia.ac.uk/ruskin/en/home/prospectus/ugpt/archaeology/.html

Institute for Archaeologists (IfA)

The IfA advances the practice of archaeology and allied disciplines by promoting professional standards and ethics for conserving, managing, understanding and promoting enjoyment of heritage. IfA is a professional organisation for all archaeologists and others involved in protecting and understanding the historic environment. There are a number of membership grades up to full membership. Entry to these grades depends on qualifications and practical experience, these include NVQ training.

Contact details: www.archaeologists.net
e-mail: membership@archaeologists.net

Archaeological Field Groups

There are two excellent voluntary field groups in Cambridge whose aims are to promote public interest in archaeology by means of fieldwork, lectures and workshops. Both groups are closely associated with the Cambridge Antiquarian Society, they are:

Cambridge Archaeology Field Group

Contact details: www.cafg.net
e-mail: cafg.may@ntlworld.com
Fen Edge Archaeology Group

Contact details: www.feag.co.uk
e-mail: feaginfo@gmail.com